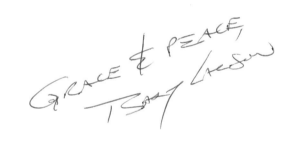

GRACE & PEACE,
T Barry Larson

Introduction

I am both a photographer as well as a hospice chaplain. [I work with the terminally ill.] Because of that I view the world differently than most. I see both beauty and heartache daily. Since working with hospice I have come to see how short and how precious life is. As with beauty, life is such a gift, something we should never take for granted.

In ministering to patients I have found that a well-timed joke or story is often just what the doctor ordered. Time and time again patients have told me how much they look forward to my visits, not only because I help them view their problems from a different perspective, but because I bring a smile to their faces. When we're able to laugh, our problems don't seem quite as bad. For example, many patients struggle with forgetfulness because of age or the strong medications they're on. I ask them, "Do you know there are three signs of old age? The first one is forgetfulness...and...uh...I can't recall the other two."—They laugh, and suddenly being forgetful isn't so bad. In this book I share some of my favorite jokes. Please take them in the kind spirit in which they're shared. Being part Swedish, being married to a Texan, and having many patients who are Catholic or Baptist, I have some Swedish, Texas, Catholic and Baptist jokes in this book. I mean no insult to any of these groups.

Besides photography, I love to write. In this book I've included numerous short stories and parables which I've written. I also love to collect provocative quotes and sayings which touch both mind and heart. It will not be hard for you to discover that C.S. Lewis, Peter Kreeft, John Eldredge, Pascal, and Bill Hybels are some of my favorite authors since the majority of quotes are from them. If this book brightens your day, lifts your spirits, or in any way draws you closer to God, then it will have served its purpose.

—Enjoy!

Scripture taken from the HOLY BIBLE, NEW INTERNATIONAL VERSION® Copyright© 1973, 1978, 1984 by International Bible Society. Used by permission of Zondervan Publishing House. All rights reserved.

ISBN-10: 0-9755001-2-0

Published by **4Seekers Publishing** in conjunction with Kingsgate Publishing.

901 Missouri Blvd., Suite144 · Jefferson City, Missouri 65109
www.4seekers.com

QUOTES FOR THIS BOOK

Over the years I have collected many quotes from many different sources. Unfortunately I didn't always write down those sources. My apologies! I can tell you that the majority of quotes come from the following books and authors. Their writings speak to both the heart and the mind. They are my all-time favorites. Of all the books I've ever read, short of scripture, I must say that *The Weight Of Glory* by C.S. Lewis has probably had the most profound impact on my thinking. It radically changed how I view people, as well as showing me that the deepest longings of my heart were for God and Heaven. Lord willing, as Lewis says, "Some day... we shall get in."

C.S. Lewis
The Weight Of Glory
Mere Christianity
The Problem Of Pain
The Chronicles Of Narnia
The Grand Miracle
The Quotable Lewis
A Grief Observed
John Eldredge
The Sacred Romance
The Journey Of Desire
Waking The Dead
Peter Kreeft
Heaven: The Heart's Deepest Longing
Making Sense Out Of Suffering
Love Stronger Than Death
Bill Hybels
Too Busy Not To Pray
Pascal
Pensées

INDEX OF STORIES

How Valuable Are You?.. Page 4
Reflections Of A Turtle... Page 8
Mom, Don't Sit There.. Page 10
What Will Heaven Be Like?.. Page 12
The Art Collector... Page 18
Desiring Heaven.. Page 20
The Broken Tail Lights.. Page 22
God And War Veterans.. Page 24
The Dog With The Broken Leg.. Page 27
You Choose The Colors... Page 36
What's Truly Important?.. Page 37
The Cracked Pot.. Page 43
Serenity Prayer [Long Version]... Page 44
A Rich Welcome Home.. Page 45
Cupped Hands... Page 49
Most Richly Blessed.. Page 52
Cinnamon And The Lion... Page 53
Do All Roads Lead To Rome?... Page 57
The Gift Of Receiving... Page 60
Case Dismissed... Page 65
God Is For Us.. Page 69
God Has Forever To Pay Back Our Losses...................... Page 71
What Cancer Cannot Do... Page 77
Self-Evident.. Page 80
A Wedding.. Page 90
Can I Pray And Expect God To Heal Me?........................ Page 93
Footprints In The Sand... Page 99
When Life Seems Unjust.. Page 101
Answering The "Why" Questions...................................... Page 102
Stepping Through the Door... Page 105
Share Your Faith With Me.. Page 111
Edward, It's Going To Be OK.. Page 139
The One I Feed The Most.. Page 141
We Live On Holy Ground.. Page 145
Chaplain's Prayer... Page 160

How Valuable Are *You?*

I used to work in a psychiatric hospital on the adolescent unit. Many of the youths I worked with had very low self-esteem. They thought they were of no value. In one of the group exercises I'd ask them whether any of them would be willing to sell me their eyes for $1,000,000. I'd tell them, *"Now, you'll be blind the rest of your lives, but at least you'll be a millionaire."* They'd all say, *"No, I'd never do that."* I'd ask, *"How many of you would be willing to sell me your right arm for $100,000?"* Again, the answer was *"No!"*—I'd then respond, *"What this tells me, then, is that each of you are already worth at least $1,100,000."*

All of us are rich beyond measure, maybe not in dollars, but in so many other ways. When was the last time you thanked God for what you *do* have? ○R

Serving *or* Seeking?

"There are only two kinds of people one may call wise: those who serve God with all their heart because they know him, or those who seek God with all their heart because they do not know him."

—Pascal

"All that is desirable in things is an image of the supremely desirable God."

—Peter Kreeft

"Joy is the serious business of heaven."

— C.S. Lewis

"*Strength comes out of solitude.*"

—Bill Hybels

"*Nothing* is so important to man as his own state, nothing is so formidable to him as eternity."
—Pascal

"*Faith* is simply believing what we have been told, believing the unbelievable: that God has the ace up His sleeve; that the worst the devil can do is to contribute unwillingly to the best God does . . ."
—Peter Kreeft

Reflections Of A Turtle
— A PARABLE —

*L*et me introduce myself. My name is Hurkermer. I'm a land turtle. While my days are filled with endless wanderings through tall grass, it gives me plenty of time to think. I sometimes wonder how I got here, and what, if any, purpose there is to my life. Not that I am complaining, mind you, but sometimes I wonder if there is more to life than eating beetles, chewing on grass and sweet clover.

I've had some close calls in my life. My mother must have known what she was doing when she put this shell on me. If it weren't for my shell, I wouldn't be talking to you now. I'd be in turtle Heaven. I've outlasted foxes, coyotes, dogs, and even a bobcat. Life in the turtle world has its dangers. I was even stepped on by a cow once. Thankfully, her hoof slid off my back, like water off a duck's back. This occurred just after a rain and her stepping on me shoved me into the mud. It took me 20 minutes of squirming and hard digging to get out of that one.

Life for us turtles tends to be tedious, slow going. Have you ever tried to push your way through grass 5-10 times taller than you are? It definitely builds stamina. I rarely feel the wind, although I can see it blowing the grass above me. I seldom have a sense of direction. I could be going in circles for all I know.

Why am I talking to you? Well, something happened to me the other day that has perplexed me to no end. It changed my life forever, and I thought maybe you could help me make sense of it.

It all began when I was pushing through the grass in search of food and water. It was a day, like any other day, when all of a sudden, as I went through this clump of grass, there before me was open space. I saw this thing, like the biggest rock you can imagine. It was smooth, gray in color, with white stripes down the middle of it. This flat rock went as far as I could see in either direction. It was the most spectacular thing I've ever seen. [I later heard that some call it a highway, whatever that is.]

For the first time in my entire life I could see more than a few inches in front of me. I had no idea that the world was so BIG! It was incredible. It was more exciting than accidentally bumping into my cousin Bertha near the swamp two years ago.

I just looked and looked and looked. Wow! It was great! The sun beating on this unending rock warmed my tummy. It almost made my little feet burn.

I was enjoying my view so much that I decided to wander a bit further out onto this strange looking rock which went forever in either direction. Then things began to happen which scared me. I had never thought much about God until then. I had always believed in God, but I guess God seemed pretty far removed from turtle life—until *that day*.

I know you may think I'm pulling your leg in what I'm about to tell you, but I am not. I'm telling the truth.—A long way away, on this slab of endless rock, I could see this big thing coming toward me at lightening speed [by turtle standards]. It was huge, tall, wide, and long. It was about a foot off the ground, had four black round things, sort of like legs, that were rolling on the ground, carrying this big box thing, whatever it was. Those black things were going faster than a horsefly chasing a horse. And this thing, whatever it was, made a noise unlike any animal I'd ever heard. It sounded like unending thunder, a dog growling, and a wind storm all at the same time. As it got closer, the noise got louder and louder.

I couldn't have gotten out of the way if I had tried, so I did the only thing I knew to do. I pulled my head in my shell and watched in utter terror. One of the big black rolling things was coming right toward me when, at the last minute, it swerved, and this huge long thing ran over the top of me without touching me. The wind from this creature almost blew me over. [Don't tell anyone, but I left a wet puddle right there on that highway!]

Was this a visitation from God or an angel? I still wonder. While I was mulling that thought over, more and more of these creatures kept coming toward me at lightning speed, most of them just barely missing me. Let me tell you, my world view has forever changed. I loved being out there on that slab of rock with the white stripes, but those things whizzing by my head scared me. If one of them had hit me, I bet I'd be dead. They were far bigger than a cow, and the ground vibrated when they went past.

Well, it didn't take long for me to figure out that I didn't belong there. I headed for the nearest grass and I plowed into it. I could still hear those creatures hours later, going up and down that never-ending rock. But eventually, I was away from there with only the sound of the crickets and bull frogs.

So, where am I now? I'm in some farmer's field sitting on a dry cow patty. It doesn't smell the greatest, but at least I can see several inches in front of me. It reminds me of that day when I could see forever. Except for the stars and sun overhead, I never get to see very far.

Something changed in me that day. While I was frightened out of my wits, I long for that view again. I yearn for a life where I can see. There is an ache in my heart to be able to walk without every step being so darn hard. On that slab of rock I went faster than I'd ever gone in my entire life. It was amazing. I felt so free.

I've heard that some animals enjoy running. I understand why now. If I could have stayed on that slab, I would have taken up running too. Maybe I could get somebody to do some bodywork on my shell and streamline it. You know, "Hot Rod Turtle."

Someday, when I get the courage, I may go in search of the never-ending rock again. Maybe one of those strange creatures will stop and give me a ride. I wonder if they would take me to where the slab ends?

Come to think of it, I wonder if it ever ends?—Oh well. A turtle can't know everything.

I know this probably sounds far fetched, but honest, this really happened to me. I'm not lying. Someday you too may encounter *Someone*, or something, unlike anything you've ever known. Will you be ready? ❧

— Love, Uncle Hurkermer

Postscript

*M*y first pet turtle as a child was named Hurkermer. In my job as a hospice chaplain, I do a lot of driving. I frequently drive past or over land turtles, always being careful not to hit them. One day driving along, I began thinking what it must be like for them, thus this short parable.

Sometimes I feel like a turtle, wandering onto the highway of life, seeing cars for the first time. When God enters our world, it is much the same way. Our lives are never quite the same. At the birth of Jesus, do you recall how the angels appeared to some shepherds in the field? I bet they felt much like Hurkermer. Do you suppose their lives were ever the same after that? No way.

Like Hurkermer, God may use the dramatic to get our attention. It may be the feeling you get as you look at the night sky and see thousands of stars, or witness the birth of a baby. Or, it may come with the death of a loved one, or being confronted with a terminal illness yourself. However it happens, we all need to be awakened to the reality of God and how short and precious life is.

"Mom, Don't Sit There."

My first year with hospice I had a young 19 year old patient with abdominal cancer. I asked her if she had come to the place in her life where, if she were to die, she knew she would go to Heaven. She said, "No." I then shared with her from Scripture the good news of God's love in Christ. She decided that she wanted to commit her life to Christ, and so we prayed together as she invited Christ to become her Lord and Savior. A real peace seemed to come over her.

The next morning her mother went into her bedroom and started to sit on her bed. She said, "Mom, don't sit there. There's an angel there."—The following morning she died.

We never know when "our day" will come, which is why the Bible reminds us, "Now is the day of salvation." (II Corinthians 6:2) Don't procrastinate! ❧

" *I tell you the truth, whoever hears my word and believes him who sent me has eternal life and will not be condemned; he has crossed over from death to life."*

—John 5:24

What Will *Heaven* Be Like?

A year or so ago I read through the New Testament and underlined every verse that had to do with Heaven. I wrote all of the verses down, organized them by topic, and here's what I found. You may find some surprises. I certainly did. I invite you to come with me on a journey where you will get a sneak preview of Heaven. Dig out your New Testament, a pen and some paper, and join me in this study. You'll have to look up the verses as there were too many to write out. In broad terms, here is what the Bible has to say about Heaven.

HEAVEN WILL BE A PLACE OF ETERNAL REST *&* PEACE

There will be nothing to make us afraid. At last, we can rest from our earthly labors and concerns [Hebrews 4:1,3, 10,11]. Interestingly, while Heaven is a place of rest, it is not necessarily a quiet place. In fact, it is often very noisy. There is thunder coming from the throne of God, great multitudes of people will be shouting and rejoicing, there are mighty angels speaking with loud voices, etc. [Hebrews 12:26; Revelation 1:13-16; 6:1; 7:10; 8:5; 10:3; 11:15,19; 14:14,15; 16:1; 18:2; 19:1,6,17,18].

BEAUTY *&* CELEBRATION

I once took a trip to Colorado to go hiking in the mountains with a friend. As we were ready to leave he said, "I hope you brought two pairs of socks." I said, "How come?" He said, "It's so beautiful up there your first pair will get knocked off!"—That is how I like to think of Heaven. We'll each need an extra pair of socks. In I Corinthians 2:9 Paul says, "No eye has seen, no ear has heard, no mind has conceived what God has prepared for those who love him."

The leaves of the New Testament rustle with tales of vibrant colors around the throne, of streets of gold, of foundations of precious jewels [Revelation 19-22]. The Bible speaks of incredible brightness and light

[versus hell which is absolute darkness: Jude 13; II Peter 2:17]. According to Paul, God dwells in "unapproachable light" [I Timothy 6:16]. The glory and brightness coming from God will fill Heaven and earth [Revelation 21:23; cf. Ezekiel 43:2 in the Old Testament]. Heaven will be filled with color and light beyond comprehension. Angelic beings and glorified saints, it says, will shine like the sun or the morning star [Matthew 4:16; 13:43; 17:2; 28:3; Mark 9:3; Luke 2:9; 9:29-31; 24:4; Acts 9:3; 12:7; 22:6,11; Ephesians 5:27; II Thessalonians 1:7; 2:8; I Peter 2:9; II Peter 1:17; I John 2:8; Revelation 1:13-16; 18:1; 21:23].

Everyone in Heaven is said to wear white [or white with gold]. What color is the embodiment of all colors? It is white. All the colors of the rainbow are in white. What one color best reflects true color? White. Imagine all God's children dressed in white, as colors from the throne of God reflect on everyone's clothing. It will be beautiful beyond words. [See: Mark 9:3; Luke 9:29-31; John 20:12; Revelation 1:13-16; 19:8; 21:3.]

We will not only see glory, but we will enter into it, bathe in it, embrace it, and rejoice in it [Matthew 24:27; 25:31; Mark 8:58; 13:26; Luke 9:26,29-31; 21:27; 24:26; John 1:14; I Corinthians 2:7-9; II Corinthians 4:16-18; Ephesians 3:16; Philippians 3:20,21; Colossians 1:27; I Timothy 1:17; II Timothy 4:18; Hebrews 1:3; 2:7,10; I Peter 5:1; II Peter 1:3; Revelation 1:6; 4:2,3; 21:19-26].

While Heaven will be beautiful beyond expression, Paul also says something very interesting. Following his vision of Heaven, Paul did not focus on what he had seen, although it had to be incredible; instead he said he "heard inexpressible things, things that man is not permitted to tell." [II Corinthians 12:4]—Paul, one of the wisest, most intelligent men to ever live, was overwhelmed by the profound wisdom and the things which were talked about in Heaven. Imagine sitting at the feet of infinite wisdom.

In Heaven there will also be joyful celebration and feasting [Matthew 8:11; Luke 12:33-37; 14:24; 22:30; Revelation 19:9]. Can you imagine sitting in glorious light, with music and angels; fellowshipping and talking with people you love

at the deepest heart-level? No superficiality. No small talk. And, if we could see each other as we will one day be, we would be tempted to fall at each others' feet and worship one another [Revelation 19:10].

INHERITANCE

When we get to Heaven we will not be bored sitting on some cloud strumming a harp. Rather, it says we will inherit a Kingdom, that we will be joint-heirs with Christ, that God will put us in charge of all he has, that we will rule with Him, and other such incredible things. For example:

a. We will be joint-heirs with Christ [Romans 8:17; Ephesians 1:18; Revelation 21:7].

b. All spiritual blessings will be ours in Christ. [Ephesians 1:3].

c. We will inherit a Kingdom [Matthew 7:21; 21:41,43; 25:34; Colossians 1:12,13; Hebrews 12:28; James 2:5].

d. We will inherit a city, the New Jerusalem, something so beautiful it defies description. It will be 1,400 miles high, wide, and long [Hebrews 11:10; 13:14; Revelation 21,22].

e. We will inherit a home [John 14:1,2]. It will be a home of righteousness. There will be no sin, pain, death, or suffering. There will be no need of police, firemen, doctors, nurses, hospitals, prisons, or other such things [II Peter 3:13; Revelation 21:3-5,27].

f. We will inherit a country [Hebrews 11:14,16].

g. We will inherit a place described as paradise [Luke 23:43]. With words that awaken our imagination, we are told that we will drink from the water of life, that we will eat from the tree of life, and that some day we will be swallowed up by life. [John 7:38; II Corinthians 5:1-4; I Timothy 6:18; I Peter 2:9; Revelation 2:6; 7:16,17; 21:6; 22:1,14,17].

h. As hard as it is to comprehend, God will put us in charge of all his possessions, which includes a New Heaven and a New Earth and over things we cannot imagine. [Matthew 24:46,47; 25:23,29; Luke 12:43,44; Romans 8:32; Galatians 3:29; Hebrews 6:12; 10:34.]

i. We will possess each other. Just as husband and wife here on earth are "one," in heaven we will all be "one," just as the holy Trinity is "one." [John 17:20,21].

In I Corinthians 3:22,23 Paul says "Whether Paul or Apollos or Cephas ... all are yours." Did you catch it? He mentions people as one of our possessions. With all the glorious people and things in Heaven, why won't we covet and lust after them?—Because they are already ours. (We don't lust or covet what we already possess.) In Heaven there will be no lust since we will all own and enjoy each other in a gloriously holy way. Such oneness and joy is hard to fathom, but so it will be.

WE WILL HAVE A GLORIOUS NEW BODY

No more wrinkles, love-handles, saddle-hips, aches or pains. We will have a glorious new body that will radiate glory and light, that will not be confined by gravity [I Thessalonians 4:17]. It will be eternal, immortal, and imperishable [Romans 8:11,18-25; I Corinthians 15:37, 42-53; II Corinthians 4:17; 5:1-4; Philippians 3:19,21; I Peter 1:4]. Our new bodies will also have incredible power. Like a seed, we were sown in weakness, but we will be raised in awesome power. [I Corinthians 15:43; Ephesians 1:19].

HEAVEN WILL BE ETERNAL

When we receive Christ as Lord and Savior, we inherit eternal life. It is hard to comprehend timelessness, where there is no night, where fullness of joy will be the order of the (endless) day, where there will be no fatigue, no boredom.

[See: Matthew 19:29; Mark 10:29,30; Luke 16:9; 18:30; John 3:16,36; 4:14,36; 5:24; 6:40; 10:28; 12:25; 17:2,3; Romans 2:6,7; 6:23; Galatians 6:8; I Thessalonians 4:17; II Timothy 1:10, 2:10; Titus 3:7; Hebrews 5:9; 9:15,28; I Peter 1:9; II Peter 1:11].18:30; John 3:16,36; 4:14,36; 5:24; 6:40; 10:28; 12:25; 17:2,3; Romans 2:6,7; 6:23; Galatians 6:8; I Thessalonians 4:17; II Timothy 1:10, 2:10; Titus 3:7; Hebrews 5:9; 9:15,28; I Peter 1:9; II Peter 1:11].

IT WILL BE A PLACE OF REWARDS

What we do on earth counts for eternity. Jesus even went so far as to say that if we give someone a cup of cold water in his name that we will not lose our reward [Mark 9:41].

a. When Christ returns for his church it says he will have his rewards with him. [Matthew 16:27; Revelation 22:12]. This is when we will get our new bodies, and our greatest reward will to be with Jesus, to finally see him face to face and become his bride.

b. Jesus taught that a major goal of our lives should be to "store up treasures in Heaven." [Matthew 6:19-21].—Jesus calls those who just lay up earthly treasure, "fools." [Luke 12:13-21]—Only those who have laid up treasure in Heaven are truly wise and rich [Matthew 5:12; 6:19-21; 19:21; Luke 12:33,34; I Timothy 6:19; Hebrews 10:35,36; I Peter 2:12; Revelation 22:12].

c. God will bring all our works into judgment, and we will be rewarded for our good deeds. If we were persecuted for the name of Christ we will receive a great reward [Luke 6:22,23]. Attitude is also important. Those with a servant's heart will be specially rewarded [Matthew 18:4; 23:12; Mark 10:43; Luke 14:11]. [Also see: Matthew 25:31-46; Luke 6:22,23; 12:37,38; 14:14; John 3:19; 6:27; I Corinthians 3:8,13,14; 4:5; 9:17; 15:58; II Corinthians 1:14; 5:10; Ephesians 6:8,10; Philippians 2:16; 3:14; Colossians 3:23,24; Hebrews 4:13; 6:10; Revelation 11:18; 14:3; 19:7,8.]

d. There are varying degrees of reward in Heaven [Matthew 5:19; 10:41; 11:11; 18:1-4; II John 8], just as there are varying degrees of punishment in hell [Matthew 10:15; 11:21,22; Mark 12:40; Luke 10:12-14]. If I read scripture correctly, those who bury their talents, and live according to the flesh, will suffer loss and embarrassment on the day of judgment. [Matthew 25:24-30; Mark 8:38; I Corinthians 3:12-15; 4:4,5; 11:11; II Corinthians 5:10; Galatians 6:7-9; James 3:1; II John 1:8]. Great reward is promised those who overcome [Revelation 2:7,10,11,17,26; 3:5,12,21].

God longs for people who will love and obey him with all their heart [I Corinthians 15:58]. They will be rewarded with "glory and honor" [Romans 2:6,7,10; I Peter 1:4,7]. Many will inherit crowns [I Corinthians 9:25; II Timothy 4:8; James 1:12]. God will praise each of us for the good we have done [I Corinthians 4:5]. Can you imagine all the eyes of Heaven upon you, and have God himself honor you by saying, "Well done!"? [See: Matthew 25:19-23; I Corinthians 4:5; Philippians 2:16; I Peter 1:7; Revelation 4:5].

If you came to Christ late in life, thank God you came. It is better late than never. Through the blood of Christ all our sins can be forgiven, even the sins of not living for God. In Christ there is forgiveness. To the best of our knowledge, we are asked to confess and repent of our sins. We are promised forgiveness. [I John 1:9; Mark 11:25; Luke 6:37; Romans 3:23; 4:7,8; 5:8; 8:1, 32; I Corinthians 11:31; I John 1:8-10; 2:1,2; 4:16-18; etc.]. It is better to finish the race of life strong, than start strong and end weak [II Timothy 4:7,8; Revelation 2:4,5].

e. Those living for Christ will be richly welcomed into Heaven [Luke 16:9; II Peter 1:11]. As I have pondered, "What would a rich welcome into the eternal kingdom of our Lord and Savior be?", I thought of several things. Obviously, to be welcomed by Jesus, as Stephen was at his death [Acts 7:55,56], would be incredible. To finally meet my guardian angel(s) will be awesome. Then I thought how wonderful it would be to have all the people whose lives I've touched, and who have touched my life, be there to greet

me.—Talk about a party and joy unspeakable.

There is a story told of an old missionary who had to return home because of health reasons. On board his ship was a famous personality. As the ship pulled into port there was a large crowd of people with banners, balloons, and a band to welcome the celebrity. As the old missionary walked down the gang plank, there wasn't a single soul there to greet him. He felt sad and terribly disappointed. He lifted his eyes toward Heaven and said, "Lord, did you forget?" The Lord replied, "My son, you're not home yet!"

g. Perhaps the greatest reward of all will be the closeness we share with God. In very colorful language the Bible speaks of us entering into the joy of the Lord [Matthew 25:23; John 15:11,12; 16:22]. As C.S. Lewis once remarked, "Joy is the serious business of Heaven."

The New Testament says that we will experience unimaginable closeness with God. He will dwell with us [Revelation 21:1-7], and he will "dwell in us" [John 14:20; II Corinthians 5:5; Ephesians 1:13,14,23; 2:21,22]. God will give us a new name [Revelation 2:17], and for all eternity we will be able to look into the face of love, into the very face of God [Revelation 22:4]. Much of Heaven will simply be searching out and enjoying who God is. He is infinite, eternal, all-powerful, all-wise, all-loving, all-holy, unchanging, etc.

With great delight, and with romance beyond all words, we, the church, will be wed to Christ [Matthew 25:1-10; Ephesians 5:31, 32; Revelation 19:6-10; 21:2]. [For other verses about our relationship with God see: Luke 10:42; 12:37,38; John 12:26; 14:1,2; 17:5, 21,22; Romans 8:29,35,37-39; I Corinthians 2:9; 13:12; 15:49; Ephesians 1:3,23; 3:8; Philippians 3:8; Colossians 2:2,3; I Peter 1:8; 5:1; Jude 24,25; Revelation 3:4,5,12,21; 22:3,4.]

HEAVEN WILL BE A PLACE OF TOTAL DISCLOSURE

One of the more unsettling aspects of Heaven is that it will be a place of total disclosure. If I understand correctly, on judgment day every thought, word, and deed will be exposed for all to see and hear [Matthew 12:36-42; Mark 4:22; Luke 12:2-9]. At first this thought scared me, and it still does some, but it will also bring relief; no more secrets, no more pretending. We will know all there is to know about each other, which also answers the question of whether we will know each other in Heaven. Yes, we will, in ways we never dreamed.

According to Scripture, believers will judge the world and angels [I Corinthians 6:2,3]. The standard we have used in judging others will be one of the standards God will use to judge us. [Matthew 7:1,2; Mark 4:24,25]. It other words, it pays to show mercy. If we have shown mercy, we can expect to receive more mercy [Matthew 5:7].

I was once speaking with a terminally ill patient and she said she didn't feel good enough to go to Heaven. I said, "You're not. That's why we need a Savior." I then told her the story of the brother and sister who had gotten their school pictures. The sister was complaining about how bad her pictures looked. She said, "These pictures don't do me justice." Her brother replied, "You don't want justice, you want mercy!"—We all stand in need of God's mercy, and that is the wonderful good news Jesus brings us. If we are willing to place our faith and trust in Him, and turn from our sins (repent), we will not only be forgiven, but we will inherit eternal life and all that I've just described.

Pascal, the 17th century French mathematician/philosopher, said, "There are only two kinds of people one may call wise: those who serve God with all their heart because they know him, or those who seek God with all their heart because they do not know him."

We cannot undo the past, with its failures, sins, and omissions, but we can accept God's forgiveness today, and begin living for him with a holy passion. We have but a short time here on earth to lay up treasure in Heaven, but all have eternity to enjoy them. As C.S. Lewis said, "When the author walks

on to the stage the play is over." I pray that you will know Christ's incredible love for you, and that this love will become the motivation for all you do [Ephesians 3:14-21]. Loving God, others, and ourselves is what it is all about. You only have one life to live for God. Don't miss this opportunity. Imagine the joy of investing in the lives of people—whether praying for them, winning them to Christ, serving them in love, discipling them—and having all eternity to enjoy them and feel their gratitude. This may be one reason Paul wrote in I Thessalonians 2:19, "For what is our hope, our joy, or the crown in which we will glory in the presence of our Lord Jesus when he comes? Is it not you?"—People! Are you investing your life in eternal relationships? [Matthew 28:19,20]. Streets of gold will be nice, but my heart aches for never-ending relationships of love.

Just as Heaven is real, so is hell. Eternal issues beyond what you or I can possibly imagine are at stake. The main purpose of life is to prepare for eternity. Each of us are one breath and one heartbeat from stepping into *forever*. Life matters, incredibly so.

If you have never committed your life to Christ, and you are not sure that if you were to die today that you would go to Heaven, may I suggest the following prayer: *"Dear Lord Jesus, I thank you for loving me. I am sorry for the sin, and pride, and lack of trust that has kept me from you. I believe you died on the cross and rose again to pay for my sin which has separated me from you. As best as I know how, right now, I place my life in your hands. I invite you to come into my life. Forgive me of my sin and make me the person you want me to be. By your grace I want to start living for you. Calm my fears, carry my burdens, and open my heart to receive your love. Thank you for hearing this prayer. Amen."*

In Colossians 3:1,2 Paul says we are to set our hearts and our minds on things above (Heaven), not on the things of this world. Once Heaven becomes real to you, as it has to me, it will change how you live. Living with an eternal perspective changes everything. We live in a little speck of time between two eternities, but oh what a speck of time it is. Enjoy it, and live it to the max for our Lord, for soon, very soon, it will all be over. ∞

—Hope to see you there!

"*The best and most beautiful things in the world cannot be seen or even touched. They must be felt with the heart.*"

—Helen Keller

The Art Collector

"Thou has made us for Thyself, and our hearts are restless until they rest in Thee."

—Augustine

The story is told of an elderly man, a widower, who had an only son. Over the years he had amassed several hundred thousand dollars of valuable paintings. It was his desire, upon his death, to leave his inheritance to his only son. However, Vietnam came along and his son got drafted. In the course of the war his son was killed. Upon hearing of his son's death, the old gentleman sank into a deep depression which lasted almost two years.

Then, one day, there was a knock at his front door. When he opened the door, there stood a rather young hippie-looking fellow with a beard and long hair. The young man said, *"Sir, you don't know me, but I served in Vietnam with your son. In fact, if it weren't for your son, I wouldn't be here today because he gave his life to save my life. Now I know you collect artwork, and while I am not a great artist, I painted a portrait of your son when I was in Nam and I would like you to have it."*

Well, sure enough, it wasn't great artwork, but it really did capture the likeness of the son. The father loved the painting so much that he took down one of his very valuable paintings above his fireplace and hung the picture of his son there. Often at night he'd have a fire going, some soft music playing, and as he'd look at the painting he would feel encouraged.

As the years went by, eventually the old art collector also died. Because there was no one to leave his inheritance to, art dealers from all around the world came to bid on his very valuable paintings which were to be auctioned off.

As the auctioneer began, he said, *"It was in the father's will, the first painting to be auctioned is the picture of his son."*—As you can imagine, no one wanted it because it wasn't great artwork, and there was silence. Eventually, the old gardener spoke up. He said, *"You know, I worked for that family for many a year and their son was like a son to me. Now, I'm not a wealthy man, but I will gladly bid $35."*

Again, there was silence. Eventually the auctioneer said, *"Going . . . Going . . . Gone!"* Then he said, *"The auction is now over!"*—There was a loud gasp and a stunned silence. The auctioneer said, *"It was in the father's will, 'Whoever receives my son, receives it all.'"*

If you have received Christ (John 1:12; Ephesians 2:8,9), then you too have *received it all* (I Corinthians 3:21,22; Ephesians 1:18).

"A wound that goes unacknowledged and unwept is a wound that cannot heal."

—John Eldredge

Desiring Heaven

*I*n one of the most powerful books I've ever read, *The Journey of Desire*, John Eldredge points out that *it is impossible to hope for that which we do not desire.* Do you long for Heaven, or does it sound like a place of total boredom? You may rightly ask, *"How can I desire a place I've never seen or been?"*—Let me address this question if I may. I truly believe that if you learn to *desire* Heaven, then you will *hope* for Heaven, and it will change the course of your life; not to mention affecting how you view life itself.

To start with, visualize the most beautiful sight you've ever seen. For me it was the summer of 1978. I'd just driven across western Kansas and eastern Colorado in rain. As I approached Denver, the storm passed, and there before me were the snow-capped Colorado Rockies. It was near sunset and the air had that fresh luminous quality. The sky seemed to be filled with every shade of purple, lavender, pink, peach, and orange you can imagine, capped with a bright red sun just above the mountain peaks. And to top it off, behind me, where the storm had just passed, was a brilliant rainbow and some geese flying south. It was so incredible that I pulled off the highway and stared. But, do you know what? Within twenty-five minutes it was gone and I felt so sad.—*"If it could have just lasted longer! If only I could have, somehow, entered into the beauty and stayed."*

Or, have you ever been to a music concert that is your type of music, whatever that might be, and for a brief while it seems as though you are suspended in time? But then what happens? The curtain drops, the lights come on, and it is over. If you're like me, a wave of sadness often hits.—Again I feel, *"If it could have just continued and not stopped!"*

Or, do you recall your first feelings of romantic love and how wonderfully exciting they were? When this person would walk past, your heart would go pitter-patter. Do you still have these wonderful feelings?—Probably not. And while you may still deeply love whomever you're with [if you are with someone], I'm guessing those feelings of romantic love have diminished. He may snore and not pick up after himself. Maybe she can't cook and wakes up in a bad mood.

Or, have you ever seen someone's face and been drawn like a magnet to it? You could seemingly stare into the beauty of that face, into the beauty of those eyes of love and acceptance, forever. And then what happens? The person gets up and leaves, or passes you by, and a knife pierces your soul.

Well, what would it be like if you could live some place where the beauty never fades, where the music never ends, where the feelings of passionate love, excitement, and adventure never diminish, and where for all eternity you could stare into the face of perfect love; the face of God?—You have just described your *desire* for Heaven.

You see, ever since you were born, God has planted the longings for Heaven in your heart. The aches, the longings, the deep desires, the passions, the thirst for adventure and acceptance, your pining for the good ole' days; they all point in one direction, and it isn't toward earth, nor to the past, but toward God and Heaven.

Like the warm aromas coming from your mother's or grandmother's kitchen when you were a child, we only get tantalizing whiffs of Heaven now. Beauty and the glory of nature, as C.S. Lewis says, are *"only the first sketch."* Paul, in I Corinthians 2:9 says, *"No eye has seen, no ear has heard, no mind has conceived what God has prepared for those who love him."*

Listen to your heart, and your heart will tell you that these longings are true. Whether you realized it or not, you've longed for God and Heaven all your life. The God-substitutes you've turned to in order to fill these longings are nothing more than man-made idols or destructive addictions. They promise much but deliver little. There is no substitute for God, which is why, in love, God claims all. He is the only game in town. Not to choose God is to choose death.

One thousand years from now it will not matter whether you lived in a shack or a million dollar mansion, whether you drove an old used Chevy or new Porsche, or if you wore the latest designer clothes, and had the best education money could buy. What will matter is: "Did you know God?" [See: Matthew 7:21-23]. To miss knowing God is to lose everything.

A person once asked, *"How much money do you think Bill Gates will leave when he dies?"* His friend responded, *"All of it!"* One of the hardest self-evident realities of life, is that we will lose everything physical at death.—We can only take with us that which is eternal in nature, the spiritual and the relational. Jim Elliot, a missionary who was martyred for his faith, may have said it best, *"He is no fool who gives what he cannot keep to gain that which he cannot lose."* ◑

The Broken Tail Lights

*Y*ears ago I read an awesome book by Richard Foster entitled, *Celebration of Discipline*. In it he mentions that God often speaks to us through circumstances. Having just read Foster's book, I suppose my spiritual antenna was out and I was more aware of my surrounding circumstances. Then something strange happened.

As I was riding my 10-speed bicycle home from work one night, it was already dark outside, and I had my bike light on when a car passed me with a broken tail light. He had his turn signal on, and with the red reflector mostly gone his blinker light almost blinded me because it was so bright. I thought to myself, *"It has been months since I've seen a car with a broken tail light."* I didn't think much more about it. Then, about 1/2 a mile down the road, a pickup passed me with a broken tail light. The next night another car passed me with a broken tail light, and two nights later another car passed me with a broken tail light.

I began praying, *"Lord, is this coincidence or are you trying to tell me something?"* As I prayed the thought hit me, *"It was the broken ones which shined the brightest."*— Sometimes it seems God allows us to be *broken* so His light can shine through us.

Not long after this I was returning from Kansas, having visited my parents. My wife and daughter were asleep and I was having a wonderful time of prayer. I had Christian music playing and I was telling God how much I loved Him and how I was willing to do anything for Him. As I prayed, a car passed me with a broken tail light. I felt as though God was saying, *"Bart, if you mean it, are you willing to pay the cost? Are you willing to be broken so that My light might shine through you?"* The breaking process has not been easy nor fun, but as Paul learned in II Corinthians 12:10, God often shines the brightest through our brokenness; *"When I am weak, then I am strong."*—If you're battling a major problem or illness, let Him shine through your brokenness. ❧

"*Miracles begin to happen...once you are convinced in the core of your being that God is willing, that He is able, and that He has invited you to come before His throne and do business in prayer.*"

—Bill Hybels

GOD & WAR VETERANS

I know a man who has a framed display of the metals he received during WWII, including the bronze star. A relative once asked him, *"What are all these metals?"* He said, *"I guess it was for killing too many Germans."* He then broke down and wept uncontrollably. As a chaplain I have worked with many war veterans: WWII, Korea, Vietnam, Gulf War, etc. I had one patient who was blown out of his foxhole twice and lived. Another landed on Normandy Beach, Day 1. All he would say was, *"You can't imagine."* Another patient of mine was at Pearl Harbor when it was bombed, another on the famous WWII airplane, the Memphis Belle. War is ugly. It is cruel. And, good men, especially the more sensitive types, live with haunting nightmares of guilt, loss, fear, regret, sadness, unforgiveness, anger, and feelings that few non-war veterans can even begin to comprehend. Sometimes normally good men do bad things during a war.

I don't understand what you've been through, but I know One who does: Jesus. The cross of Jesus Christ addresses the main needs of the war veteran. If you are a veteran, do you feel the need for forgiveness? Christ shed his blood to atone and pay for all your sins. Can God forgive the "big" sins? Yes. In fact, the three main writers of the Bible were all guilty of murder: Moses, David, and the Apostle Paul.

Once, when working in a psychiatric hospital, I was playing pool with a young man who had been in Satanism. He looked up me, grew very solemn and said, *"Do you think God can ever forgive me because I was present when we killed* (sacrificed) *a baby?"*—My heart hit the floor, and then I felt God gave me an answer. I replied, *"If God is big enough to forgive us for the death of Jesus, then He is big enough to forgive you for the death of that baby."* We then prayed and he asked Jesus to forgive him.

Have you been sinned against? Has your heart been broken? Are you in need of emotional and spiritual healing? At the cross you will find a Savior who can meet you in your deepest pain because he too has suffered. There is scarcely any type of emotional, physical, or spiritual pain you can imagine that Jesus has not experienced [anger, abuse, abandonment, pain, etc.]. He understands what you've been through. If you are willing to come to him you can find both forgiveness and healing. If you have been carrying guilt, pain and anger all these years, don't you think it is time to lay them down? I encourage you to pray the following prayer, or use it as a starting point for some prayers of your own.

"Dear Lord Jesus,

I have carried the sins and pains of war too long. I have tried to bury my feelings of guilt, anger and unforgiveness, but when I bury them I bury them alive, and they still live in my mind. Lord, I need you. I ask you to forgive me for all of the sins I have ever committed, especially when I was in the war. You say in your Word that if I confess my sins to you that you are faithful and just and will forgive my sins and purify me from all unrighteousness [I John 1:9]. I claim this forgiveness right now through your shed blood, Lord Jesus.

I also ask, Lord, that you not only remove the guilt, anger, and unforgiveness I've carried all these years, but I ask that you begin to heal my wounded, shattered heart. Lord, only you know the depth of my pain. I know that on the cross You bore the pain of the world. Bear my pain for me. Speak your truth into my heart. As best as I know how, right now, I receive your grace and forgiveness. Please fill me with your Holy Spirit, and help me to live a life pleasing to you. Thank you for hearing this prayer. ❧

Amen."

—May his grace, mercy, and peace be yours.

"*God's power flows primarily to people who pray. . .*
when we work, we work, but when we pray, God works . . ."

—Bill Hybels

The Dog With The Broken Leg

Before we bought our first house, my wife and I lived in a mobile home in the country. One day when we got home from work there was the cutest little dog in our front yard with a broken back leg. She had obviously been hit by a car. We searched and searched for the owner, but no one claimed her. Since we didn't own a dog we decided to pay a vet $100 to pin her broken leg rather than have her put to sleep. You might say we redeemed her life. We named her Dusty and she became part of the household. She looked like a small version of Walt Disney's "*Shaggy Dog.*" We loved her.

However, one evening as we arrived home from work we realized that we'd forgotten to let her outside for the day. As we walked in the trailer it looked as though it had been vandalized—by a dog! We had a fluffy pillow which she'd torn up. There was fluff all over the trailer. She had peed and pooped on the carpet. She'd gotten into our collection of records (way before tapes and CD's) and chewed up many of them. It looked like a war zone. I couldn't believe it. I don't get angry easily, but I was mad. I rolled up a news paper, grabbed her by the scruff of the neck, rubbed her nose in the messes, spanked her with the newspaper, and tossed her out the front door. I was thinking to myself, "*Is she even worth keeping?*"— And then, being the pragmatic guy I am, I thought, "*No, I've paid too much for her.*"

Then it hit me. I thought about the price God had paid to redeem me. He became a man in the person of Jesus Christ and shed His own blood to purchase my salvation (Acts 20:28). Then I thought of the parallel, "*Do you suppose God will disown me the first time I 'mess' up?*" And the answer was, "*Of course not, He paid too much for me.*" He may discipline me (Hebrews 12), but He will never disown me (Hebrews 13:5, John 10:28). I'm His. He paid the ultimate price for me...and you! ❧

"*D*o not cast me away when I am old; do not forsake me when my strength is gone."

—Psalm 71:9

A hospice nurse I work with asked a 105 year old patient where she was born. The elderly lady thought and thought. Finally she said, *"I don't remember, but that was over 100 years ago!"*

A husband and wife had each died and gone to Heaven. As they were walking the streets of Heaven one day the husband couldn't get over how beautiful everything was: the presence of God, and all the angels, and choirs, and all the colors. Finally, he turned to his wife and said, "Honey, do you recall down on earth how you had us eat all that health food stuff? You know, no fried chicken, no gravy, and all that green stuff?" The wife said, "Yes." Finally the husband said, "Do you realize we could have been here about 10 years earlier if you wouldn't have done that!"

There was a widow and a widower who met one day on a park bench at a retirement home. They'd never met before and as they talked it was like two long lost friends meeting. They had a wonderful afternoon. They were both from the Midwest. Each had good first marriages and wonderful families. They had the same religious and political beliefs. They were like two peas in a pod. Near the end of the afternoon, having had such an enjoyable afternoon, the old gentlemen knelt in front of the lady. He said, "I have two questions for you. I know this first one is rather sudden, but will you marry me?" The woman was quite taken back, but upon reflection said, "Well, well, yes I will!—What's your second question?" The old gentleman replied, "Will you help me up?"

An elderly couple had been to the doctor. Because they were getting so forgetful the doctor told them to be sure and write everything down. One night the husband was going out to the kitchen. The wife said, *"Honey, while you're out there, would you get me a bowl of ice cream?"* He said, *"Why sure!"* She said, *"Now write it down."* He said, *"Oh, I'll remember."* She said, *"And Honey, while you're there, would you put some chocolate syrup and peanuts on it?"* He said, *"No problem!"* She said, *"Now write it down!"* He said, *"Oh, I'll remember."* About 15 minutes later he brings her some bacon and eggs. She looks down and says, *"You forgot the toast!"*

"A 102 year old lady was asked what the best thing was about being 102. She thought and then said, "No peer pressure!"

A woman with a terminal illness was talking with her pastor. Being very brave and confident of her own salvation she was joyfully making her own funeral arrangements. She wanted everything to be just right. She told the pastor the hymns she wanted to have sung, who was to sing, the order of the service, the passages of scriptures to be read, etc. As the pastor was leaving she said, "By the way pastor, I have one more request. I'd like to be buried with a kitchen fork in my hand." The pastor looked at her with a puzzled look. She said, "When I was a small child and attended the church potluck socials, the ladies of the church would always come around and gather up all the plates. They'd always say, 'Save your forks.' I always knew that meant there was cake or pie yet to come. Now, when folks ask why I have that fork in my hand you tell them that it is a reminder that the best is yet to come."

I asked a retired friend of mine if he was as busy now that he had retired. "Well," he said, "I have half as much to do, but it takes me twice as long to do it."

Ole had been to the doctor and he said, "Doc, I think Lena is getting hard of hearing. Is there any way we can test her hearing without her knowing about it?" The doc thought and said, "Tonight when you go home, as you go in the front door, you yell out, 'Lena, I'm home. What's for supper?' If she doesn't hear you, you go to the next room and say, 'Lena, I'm home. What's for supper?' If she still doesn't hear you, you go out near the kitchen and say, 'Lena, I'm home. What's for supper?'— That way, you can gauge how her hearing is." Ole thought that sounded good, so that evening as he stepped in the front door he said, 'Lena, I'm home. What's for supper?' He didn't hear anything, so he went a little closer and said, 'Lena, I'm home. What's for supper?' He still didn't hear anything, so he went out near the kitchen and said, 'Lena, I'm home. What's for supper?' She said, "Ole, I told you three times we're having meatloaf!"

I have an elderly friend named Grover who is up in his 80's. He is a real character and loves a good joke. Recently he had to have cataract surgery done on his eyes. He told me that cataract surgery is nothing more than the doctor making a small incision across the top of each eye, removing the fluid in front of the pupil which turns yellow with age, inserting a small piece of clear plastic to replace the fluid and stitching them in place. Being a widower he had begun dating another elderly woman. Following the surgery he told her, "Here all this time I thought I had been dating a blonde!"

I had an old German Catholic patient of mine tell me, *"There are three stages in life: youth, middle age, and lookin' pretty good."* He then said, *"You're lookin' pretty good!"*

The grandkids bought grandma a Bible commentary for Christmas. Usually, the grandmother was very prompt in sending thank you notes. However, weeks went by and they didn't hear a word from grandma. So one of them finally asked her, "Well, Grandma, how are you liking the Bible commentary we gave you?" She said, "Well, to be real honest, it was very hard to read at first. But, do you know, the Bible sure sheds a lot of light on it." ✆

We all are getting older. We can fight it, or accept it and find the humor in it.

" We do not want merely to see beauty, though, God knows,
even that is bounty enough.
We want something else which can hardly be put into words—
to be united with the beauty we see, to pass into it, to receive it into ourselves,
to bathe in it, to become part of it . . .
We cannot mingle with the splendors we see.
But all the leaves of the New Testament are rustling with the
rumor that it will not always be so.
Some day, God willing, we shall get in." ∞

—C.S. Lewis from *The Weight of Glory*

TEXAS HUMOR

My wife is from Texas, and I've always gotten a kick out of Texas jokes. I hope you find these as funny as I do—BL

A Missourian drove to Texas to visit a wealthy friend. The Texan tried to impress the Missourian with how big his ranch was. He said, *"Do you know that I can get in my car and can drive for a whole day in any direction and never get off my own land."* The Missourian responds, *"You know, I've got a car just like that!"*

A young Texan moved to Oklahoma and bought a ranch. The boy's father from Texas drove up to visit. The son was proudly showing the dad around the ranch when a jackrabbit ran across the road. The father said, *"What's that thing?"* The kid said, *"Dad, that's a jackrabbit."* The father responded, *"Well in Texas they're sure a lot bigger than that!"* A while later they saw a buffalo standing in a field. The father asks, *"What's that?"* The son responds, *"Dad, that's a buffalo."* The father said, *"Well in Texas they're sure a lot bigger than that!"* A bit later, while driving near a creek, they came upon a huge snapping turtle beside the road. The father asks, *"Well, what's that?"* The son responds, *"A wood tick."*

A northerner is talking with a Texan and asks if he owns any land. The old Texan says, *"Yeah, I have a little 5 acre spread."* The northerner says, *"That's not very big."* The Texan responds, *"That's in downtown Dallas!"* ❧

"*God whispers in our pleasures but shouts in our pains.*
Pain is His megaphone to rouse a dulled world..."

—C.S. Lewis

"God always gives the best to those who leave the choice with Him."

—Unknown

"*If I find in myself a desire which no experience in this world can satisfy, the most probable explanation is that I was made for another world.*"

—C.S. Lewis from *Mere Christianity*

"*I*magine God appeared to you and said, 'I'll make a deal with you if you wish. I'll give you anything and everything you ask: pleasure, power, honor, wealth, freedom, even peace of mind and a good conscience. Nothing will be a sin; nothing will be forbidden; and nothing will be impossible for you. You will never be bored and you will never die. Only, you shall never see My face.' —Did you notice that unspeakable chill in your deepest heart at those last words? . . . your deepest mind, which knows your deepest desire, knows it: you want God more than everything else in the world."

—Peter Kreeft

"*D*o not let your hearts be troubled. Trust in God; trust also in me. In my Father's house are many rooms; if it were not so, I would have told you. I am going there to prepare a place for you. And if I go and prepare a place for you, I will come back and take you to be with me that you also may be where I am."

—John 14:1-3

You Choose The Colors

*I*f you take any photograph or painting, no matter how beautiful, if you can find the right matting and frame to put around it, it will make the picture look twice as pretty. In like manner, I believe God has put a frame around each of our lives, and that is death. At first we hate the frame, but once we accept it, the picture inside becomes more precious and beautiful.

There is a joy and a peace that comes when we accept what God has given us, no matter how difficult. Fanny Crosby, whose hymns have touched millions, became blind as a very young girl. She is the one who wrote such classic hymns as *What A Friend We Have In Jesus.* She was once asked by Dwight L. Moody, the great American evangelist, *"Fanny, if God were to grant you one wish on this earth what would it be?"*—He expected her to say, *"I'd like to receive my sight back."* Instead she said, *"I'd ask to remain blind the rest of my life so that the first face I see will be the face of Jesus."*

Attitude is one of the few things in life we can choose. You may not always be able to choose what goes inside your frame, but you can, so to speak, choose the color of the frame. ❧

What's Truly IMPORTANT?

I know no promise that He will accept a deliberate compromise. For He has, in the last resort, nothing to give us but Himself . . . For He claims all, because He is love and must bless. He cannot bless us unless He has us. When we try to keep within us an area that is our own, we try to keep an area of death. Therefore, in love, He claims all. There's no bargaining with Him . . . 'If you have not chosen the Kingdom of God, it will make in the end no difference what you have chosen instead.' Those are hard words to take.

Will it really make no difference whether it was women or patriotism, cocaine or art, whisky or a seat in the Cabinet, money or science? Well, surely no difference that matters. We shall have missed the end for which we are formed and rejected the only thing that satisfies. Does it matter to a man dying in a desert by which choice of route he missed the only well?" ଔ

—C.S. Lewis from *The Weight of Glory*

"*Blessed are they whose transgressions are forgiven, whose sins are covered. Blessed is the man whose sin the Lord will never count against him.*"

—Romans 4:7,8

"*I* consider that our present sufferings are not worth comparing with the glory that will be revealed in us. The creation waits in eager expectation for the sons of God to be revealed. For the creation was subjected to frustration, not by its own choice, but by the will of the one who subjected it, in hope that the creation itself will be liberated from its bondage to decay and brought into the glorious freedom of the children of God. We know that the whole creation has been groaning as in the pains of childbirth right up to the present time. Not only so, but we ourselves, who have the firstfruits of the Spirit, groan inwardly as we wait eagerly for our adoption as sons, the redemption of our bodies. For in this hope we were saved. But hope that is seen is no hope at all. Who hopes for what he already has? But if we hope for what we do not yet have, we wait for it patiently."

—Romans 8:18-25

"*How many of your plans take an unending future into account?*"

—John Eldredge

"*So do not throw away your confidence; it will be richly rewarded. You need to persevere so that when you have done the will of God, you will receive what he has promised.*"

—Hebrews 10:35,36

"*A*bove all else, guard your heart, for it is the wellspring of life"

—Proverbs 4:23

THE CRACKED POT

"A friend passed this story along to me. I hope that it encourages you as much as it has me." —BL

A water bearer in India had two large pots, each hung on the end of a pole he carried across his neck. One of the pots had a crack in it, while the other pot was perfect in every way. It always delivered a full portion of water at the end of the long walk from the stream to the master's house, while the cracked pot only delivered half a pitcherful of water.

For a full two years this went on daily, with the bearer delivering only one and a half pots full of water to his master's house. One day, to the surprise of the servant, the broken pot spoke. It said, *"I am so ashamed and I want to apologize to you."*

"Why?" asked the bearer. *"What are you ashamed of?"*

"I have been able, for these past two years, to deliver only half my load because this crack in my side causes water to leak out all the way back to your master's house. Because of my flaws, you have to do all of this work, and you don't get full value from your efforts," the pot said.

The water bearer felt sorry for the old cracked pot, and in his compassion he said, *"As we return to the master's house, I want you to notice the beautiful flowers along the path."*

Indeed, as they went up the hill, the old cracked pot took notice of the sun warming the beautiful wild flowers on the side of the path, and this cheered it some. But at the end of the trail, it still felt bad because it had leaked out half its load, and so again it apologized to the bearer for its failure.

The bearer said to the pot, *"Did you notice that there were flowers only on your side of your path, but not on the other pot's side?"*

"That's because I have always known about your flaw, and I took advantage of it. I planted flower seeds on your side of the path, and every day while we walk back from the stream, you've watered them.

"For two years I have been able to pick these beautiful flowers to decorate my master's table. Without you being just the way you are, he would not have this beauty to grace his house."

Each of us has our own unique flaws. We're all cracked pots. But if we will allow it, the Lord will use our flaws to grace His Father's table.

In God's great economy, nothing goes to waste.

So as we seek ways to minister together, and as God calls you to the tasks He has appointed for you, don't be afraid of your flaws. Acknowledge them, and allow Him to take advantage of them, and you, too, can be the cause of beauty on His pathway.

Go out boldly, knowing that in our weakness we find His strength, and that *"In Him every one of God's promises is a 'Yes.'"* ❧

Serenity Prayer

{long version}

God grant me the Serenity to accept

the things I cannot change,

Courage to change the things I can, and

Wisdom to know the difference.

Living one day at a time,

enjoying one moment at a time.

Accepting hardship as a pathway to peace.

Taking, as Jesus did, this sinful world as it is,

not as I would have it.

Trusting that You will make all things

right if I surrender to your will.

So that I may be reasonably happy in

this life, and supremely happy with

You forever in the next.

—Amen.

A Rich Welcome Home

There is a story told about an old missionary who had faithfully served the Lord overseas. His health had deteriorated and he was having to return to the States to spend his last few years. He came across the ocean on a huge ocean liner. It so happened that there was a very famous celebrity aboard the ship. As it pulled into the harbor, there was a large crowd of people there to greet the celebrity with banners and balloons. As the old missionary hobbled down the gangplank, there wasn't a single soul there to greet him. He felt so discouraged and looking up to Heaven said, *"Lord, did you forget?"*—The Lord said, *"My son, you're not Home yet!"*

The verse II Peter 1:11 talks about those committed to the Lord's work receiving a "rich welcome into the eternal kingdom of our Lord and Savior..."

I started thinking, "What would a rich welcome be? Obviously, to have the Lord welcome me with open arms would be joy beyond measure, and then I thought of all the hospice patients I've known who have died. I got to thinking, *Wouldn't it be awesome if many of the hundreds of patients I've known and worked with were there to greet me as I enter Heaven?"* Talk about a joyous homecoming. ❧

"*Because we love something else more than this world, we love even this world better than those who know no other.*"

—C.S. Lewis

"*B*e still and know that I am God."

—Psalm 46:10

" *W*e find in his [Jeremiah's] writings a most disturbing answer to the question: Why do bad things happen to good people? It is that there are no 'good people.' The puzzle should rather be why good things happen to bad people! We are good people only by the standards of bad people."

—Peter Kreeft

"'Thy will be done'
is the infallible road
to total joy."

—Peter Kreeft

CUPPED HANDS

Several years ago, while working on an adolescent unit in a psychiatric hospital, I was counseling with an eleven year old boy who had been sexually abused. He was also picked on by the kids at school. In short, this little guy had a tough life, and my heart went out to him. However, having talked with him, I knew he believed in God. So, one day I asked him to cup his hands, as though he was holding water, and I asked him to pretend to put all of the anger, and the hurt, and the rejection, and the worry and the fear—everything he was feeling—into his hands and feel how heavy it was. He said, *"Yeah, it weighs a lot!"*

I then asked him to pretend that God's hands were under his, and when he could, to open his hands and dump all of these weighty issues and feelings into God's hands. I told him that what he was carrying was too heavy for him; that only God was strong enough to carry his load. He said he'd give it a try.

The next morning when I went onto the adolescent unit, he came running up to me smiling ear to ear. He said, *"It works!"*—And it does. —I don't know what burdens you are carrying today: fear, worry, anger, bitterness, hurt, rejection, disappointment, a wounded heart . . . What I can tell you is that there is Someone who longs to carry your burdens; Jesus.

He said, *"Come to me, all you who are weary and burdened, and I will give you rest. Take my yoke upon you and learn from me, for I am gentle and humble in heart, and you will find rest for your souls, For my yoke is easy and my burden is light."* [Matthew 11:28-30].

The question is, *"Will you come?"*—Will you come to the One who created you? [John 1:10-12; Hebrews 1:1,2] Will you come to the One who loves you and died for you? [John 3:16; Romans 5:8, 6:23] Are you willing to place not only your problems into God's hands, but even more importantly, are you willing to place your very life into the hands of God? He loves you and will be there for you.

If you have never committed your life to Jesus Christ, or feel the need of making sure, may I suggest the following prayer?

"Dear Lord Jesus,
I thank You for loving me. I am sorry for the sin, and pride, and lack of trust that has kept me from You. I believe You died on the cross and rose again to pay for my sin which has separated me from You. As best as I know how, right now, I place my life in Your hands. I invite You to come into my life. Forgive me of my sin and make me the person You want me to be. Calm my fears, carry my burdens, and open my heart to receive your love. Thank You for hearing this prayer. Amen." ❧

— May His peace be yours.

"We may ignore, but we can nowhere evade, the presence of God.
The world is crowned with Him."

—C.S. Lewis

"The Lord is close to the brokenhearted and saves those who are crushed in spirit."

—Psalm 34:18

MOST RICHLY BLESSED

This poem was supposedly found in the pocket of a
slain Confederate soldier during the Civil War.—BL

*I asked God for strength that I might achieve.
I was made weak that I might
learn humbly to obey.*

*I asked God for health that I might do greater
things. I was given infirmity that
I might do better things.*

*I asked for riches that I might be happy.
I was given poverty that I might be wise.*

*I asked God for power that I might have the
praise of men. I was given weakness that
I might feel the need of God.*

*I asked for all things that I might enjoy life.
I was given life that I might enjoy
all things.*

*I got nothing that I asked for—but
everything I had hoped for.
Almost despite myself, my unspoken prayers
were answered.*

I am among all men most richly blessed.

Cinnamon & The Lion

One Christmas my wife and two daughters flew to Texas to see my mother-in-law, while I drove to Kansas to see my parents who live in a small country town. Because there was no one to watch our dog, Cinnamon, I took him with me. He loved all the special attention he received from my parents: the Christmas goodies, yummy leftovers, and tummy rubs.

Later in the evening, around 9:00 P.M., I decided to take Cinnamon for a short walk around the block. I decided to walk down Main Street and look at the buildings which had been so familiar to me as a child growing up. In front of the Community Center is a life-size sculpture of a lion standing on the sidewalk with its mouth open. The inside of its mouth had even been painted red to make it look realistic.

As we strolled, Cinnamon seemed to be having the time of his life, tugging at the leash, and leaving his scent on fire hydrants and lamp posts. He was pulling hard on the leash until he got about 15 feet from the sculpture. All of a sudden he froze in his tracks as he looked at the lion with its gaping mouth and white teeth showing in the dark.

Cinnamon, normally a brave dog, began walking around behind me never taking his eyes off the lion for even a second. As we proceeded to stroll past the lion, Cinnamon walked as far away from the lion as the leash would allow. Even after we were past the sculpture he had his head craned backwards looking at the lion just to be sure it wasn't going to attack. He seemed much relieved when we were well past its intimidating presence, and were safe inside my parents' home.

I laughed and laughed as I watched the whole episode unfold and told my parents about it. Then I thought how typical this is. We're all a bit like Cinnamon. Life is full of things which appear real, frightening, and far more powerful than we are. No wonder that we try to get as far away from them as possible. I sometimes wonder if God laughs because He sees our fears for what they really are: stone lions.—Isn't this where faith comes in, trusting God even when things don't make sense and we're scared spitless?

Was God in control of the world before you were born?—Yes. Will God still be in control of the world long after you're gone?—Of course. So, why don't we hand over our here-and-now fears to Him? After all, He is the One who longs to walk beside us, to protect us, and lead us safely Home.

What are the lions in your life? You can focus your attention and your gaze on the lions in your life, or you can look to the One who said, "Never will I leave you; never will I forsake you."

Dear Lord Jesus, watch over us and protect us. Grant us the grace to humbly seek you. Deliver us from the stone lions in our lives. ❧

—Amen

Photo of our dog Cinnamon.

"*Most* people are about as happy as they make up their minds to be."

—Abe Lincoln

"*W*hat would it be to taste at the fountainhead, that stream of which even these lower reaches prove so intoxicating? Yet that, I believe, is what lies before us. The whole man is to drink joy from the fountain of joy."

—C.S. Lewis, from *The Weight of Glory*

"*Of course he isn't safe. But he's good.*"

—Referring to Aslan, the Christ-figure
in C.S. Lewis' books, *The Chronicles Of Narnia*

"*D*ealing with the living God is a little like a nuclear war: it can upset your whole day."

—Peter Kreeft

A Hospice Prayer

"Lord, whenever the time comes in my life that I can bring You greater glory through my death than through my life, then I want You to take me, but not before.

—*Amen."*

Do All Roads Lead To Rome?

*I*t is rather fashionable in our day of tolerance and political correctness to say that it doesn't really matter what one believes about God as long as one is sincere. After all, don't all roads lead to Rome? Don't all religions lead to the same God?

I see a couple of dangers with this type of thinking: the first is simply the matter of truth. It is possible to be sincere but sincerely wrong. As a lady from Europe once told me. *"All roads don't lead to Rome. I know. I've gotten lost driving there."*—When it comes to God, the major world religions say contradictory things about God. Some say He is *one*, others that God is three-in-one, still others that God is millions of *gods*, or that we're all God. Some say God is personal, and others that He is impersonal, etc. Logically speaking, they can't all be right. With so many religions, and major differing views regarding God, who's to say who or what God is really like? Which God will you meet after death?—What is God *really* like? Who's to say?—There is actually a very simple answer. The only One who can say for sure who and what God is like is God. This is an important point to grasp. Only God can give the final word on Himself.

Now, let's suppose that one day a man stands up and boldly proclaims, "To clear up all the confusion about God, I want you to know that *I AM* God! *(John 8:58). I am THE way, THE truth and THE life!"* (cf., John 14:6). This gets into the verifiable. Anyone claiming to be God would be one of three things: psychotic with delusions of grandeur, a deceiver out to pull off the greatest hoax of all time, or he would be God. What if God chose to write Himself into His own story and become a man? This is the staggering claim the New Testament makes concerning Jesus. [See: John 1:1-14; 8:58; 10:28-30; 14:7-9; 20:28; Philippians 2:6-11; Colossians 1:15-20; Hebrews 1:8, etc.]

Jesus' resurrection from the dead, the reliability of the witnesses, the miracles He performed, His character, and teachings all attest and prove He was/is who He claimed to be. There are nearly one hundred prophecies about Jesus' first coming including where he was to be born (Micah 5:2), that he would die having his hands and feet pierced (Psalm 22:16; cf., Isaiah 53; Zechariah 12:10), and even the exact week and year He would die. (Daniel 9:25,26). To take a middle-of-the-road position concerning Christ is to totally fail to grasp the claims He made. Just as no one is ever half pregnant (either they're pregnant or they're not), in like manner, either Jesus is God or He isn't. There is no middle ground.

C.S. Lewis is right when he says, *"A man who was merely a man and said the sort of things Jesus said would not be a great moral teacher. He would either be a lunatic—on a level with the man who says he is a poached egg—or else he would be the Devil of Hell. You must make your choice. Either this man was, and is, the Son of God: or else a madman or something worse. You can shut Him up for a fool, you can spit at Him and kill Him as a demon; or you can fall at His feet and call Him Lord and God. But let us not come with any patronizing nonsense about His being a great human teacher. He has not left that open to us. He did not intend to."* [From *Mere Christianity*]

If you've never considered the radical claims of Christ, I urge you to do so. Faith is only as good as the object of that faith. All the faith in the world, if it is based on a lie, won't get you where you want to go. ଔ

The 23rd Psalm

"The LORD is my shepherd,
I shall not be in want.
He makes me lie down in green pastures,
he leads me beside quiet waters,
he restores my soul.
He guides me in paths of
righteousness for his name's sake.
Even though I walk through the valley
of the shadow of death,
I will fear no evil,
for you are with me;
your rod and your staff,
they comfort me.
You prepare a table before me
in the presence of my enemies.
You anoint my head with oil;
my cup overflows.
Surely goodness and love [mercy]
will follow me all the days of my life,
and I will dwell in the house of the
LORD forever."

If you can honestly say in your heart that
the first five words of this Psalm are true
for you, that the Lord is your *shepherd*, then
the rest of this Psalm is automatically true, for
it is up to the shepherd to lead the
sheep. Life becomes His worry, not yours.

Trust the Shepherd. —BL

"Therefore we do not lose heart. Though outwardly we are wasting away, yet inwardly we are being renewed day by day. For our light and momentary troubles are achieving for us an eternal glory that far outweighs them all. So we fix our eyes not on what is seen, but on what is unseen. For what is seen is temporary, but what is unseen is eternal."

—II Corinthians 4:16-18

"The glory of the Lord, is... beyond all experience and all descriptions, all categories, a beauty before which all earthly splendors, marvelous as they are, pale into insignificance."

—Thomas Dubay from *The Evidential Power of Beauty*

"Trust in him at all times, O people; pour out your hearts to him, for God is our refuge."

—Psalm 62:8

The Gift of *Receiving*

*A*re you the kind of person who is primarily a *giver* or a *taker?* If you're a *giver,* you probably feel compelled to give to others. Having to ask others for help because you're growing old, sick, or are handicapped is probably a hard pill for you to swallow. You hate it.

While this may also come as a blow to your pride, do you realize that **receiving can also be a form of giving?** Were you to look back over the years of your life, I bet there have been many people who wanted to give to you, but you, being the giver you are, found it hard to receive from them.—True? Well, now is your opportunity to allow them to give to you, especially those to whom you have given so much. You can now give them the *gift of giving*, by being willing to *receive* their love and help.

The apostle Paul in the New Testament wrote, *"Carry each other's burdens, and in this way you will fulfill the law of Christ."* [Galatians 6:2]. This verse implies that bearing *each other's* burdens is a two-way street. You bear theirs. They bear yours. Now it is your turn to receive.

Allow me to address two areas where it is imperative that you allow others to bear your burdens. The first is emotionally. People are not mind readers. How can they help you bear your emotional burdens—the fear, the discouragement, the feelings of helplessness and hopelessness, the anger, the shame, the regrets, the guilt, the humiliation—unless you share those feelings with them?

Do you remember your mother or grandmother having an old pressure cooker with the lock-lid and the little pressure release valve on top? Unless the cooker lets off steam, it will explode. Emotions are a lot like that pressure cooker. You don't want to hold your feelings in until you explode or have a breakdown. The ideal way is to let off the pressure a little bit at a time, so the pressure inside is manageable.

What am I saying? Don't hold your feelings in. Share them with others.

According to the Bible, as you allow others to *bear your burdens*, you are fulfilling the very *law of Christ.* Plus, how do you expect others to share their burdens with you if you never share your burdens with them? By sharing your burdens, you give them permission to share their burdens with you.—Remember, what you don't share, you keep.

Where and how do you start? What do you say?—How about telling a trusted friend, *"Do you have a minute? I've been **feeling** (fill in the blank: <u>scared, tired, hurt, angry, worried, overwhelmed, etc.</u>) and I just need you to **listen**. I'm not looking for advice. I know there are no easy answers, but will you let me get some stuff off my chest?"*—Pick this person wisely. The last thing you want is to pick someone who is a gossip, or who'll give you a bunch of pat answers, try to "fix" you, or will tell you, "Snap out of it."

There is a second area where you can allow others to give to you, and that is physically. Maybe you've come to the place where others are having to feed you, or, God forbid, change your *Depends* [diapers]. How humiliating! On a feeling level, it can't get much worse than that. It is at this point that most *givers* lose it and become depressed. Why? Because behind most *givers* are the hidden feelings: *"I must give love in order to receive love." "I'm unworthy to receive others' love."* You become anxious if you can't give. I know—these are the feelings I've struggled with all my life.

But is that the *law of Christ*? No? Christ was *both* a giver and a receiver. Read the New Testament and notice how many times Jesus allowed others to give to him: meals, free lodging, anointing his head with oil, washing his feet, and even carrying the cross which had become too burdensome for him to carry.—My point? Jesus knows what you are going through, and he has modeled for you that it is OK to receive. And do you know what? His love for you doesn't change one bit. In fact, as you are able to begin receiving from others, with no way of paying them back; maybe, for the first time in your life, God's unconditional love will become real to you. It may finally sink in that you don't have to be a giver in order to receive others' love and God's love. His type of love is unconditional.

As strange as it may sound, this may be one of the greatest gifts God has ever given to you. Am I saying that becoming dependent on others is a blessing in disguise? That is exactly what I am saying. And, before you write me off as crazy, please listen. According to the Bible, God's greatest gift to us, namely our salvation, is because of his grace. Grace is defined as receiving something we don't deserve. [Please read: John 1:12, 3:16; Romans 3:23; 5:8, and Ephesians 2:8,9.]

Don't let pride, the cardinal sin of all sins, stand in the way of your receiving God's love and grace. Sometimes he sends his love through other people. As you allow yourself to receive love from others, you will be better able to receive the love of the One who was nailed to a Roman cross for you. In other words, as you give yourself permission to *receive*, you open yourself to the love of Christ. It is called grace.

The issue is whether you will allow yourself to receive this love. God and others have gifts to give you, but you must be willing to humble yourself and allow them the gift of giving to you. If the roles were reversed, would you want to give to them? Probably so. So, allow them to give to you. Am I saying you're to allow them to give to you for their good? Yes, but also do it for yourself. Sometimes pride must die in order that the seeds of God's unconditional love can grow in our hearts. That's what grace is all about: receiving what we don't deserve. ❧

The Times asked a number of writers for essays on the topic
"What's Wrong with the World?" Chesterton's reply is
the shortest and most to the point in history:

"Dear Sirs: I am. Sincerely yours, G.K. Chesterton"

" *When* you painted on earth…it was because you caught glimpses of Heaven the in earthly landscape."

—C.S. Lewis from *The Great Divorce*

SEEING EACH OTHER AS IMMORTAL

The load, or weight, or burden of my neighbor's glory should be laid on my back, a load so heavy that only humility can carry it . . . to remember that the dullest and most uninteresting person you can talk to may one day be a creature which, if you say it now, you would be strongly tempted to worship, or else a horror and a corruption such as you now meet, if at all, only in a nightmare. All day long we are, in some degree, helping each other to one or other of these destinations . . . There are no *ordinary* people. You have never talked to a mere mortal. Nations, cultures, arts, civilizations—these are mortal, and their life is to ours as the life of a gnat. But it is immortals whom we joke with, work with, marry, snub, and exploit—immortal horrors or everlasting splendors . . . We must play. But our merriment must be of that kind (and it is, in fact, the merriest kind) which exists between people who have, from the outset, taken each other seriously . . . Next to the Blessed Sacrament itself, your neighbor is the holiest object presented to your senses."

—C.S. Lewis from *The Weight of Glory*

HOPE OF JOY

"What would it be to taste at the fountainhead that stream of which even these lower reaches prove so intoxicating? Yet that, I believe, is what lies before us. The whole man is to drink joy from the fountain of joy."

—C.S. Lewis from *The Weight of Glory*

"Perhaps the reason we are sharing in a suffering we do not understand is because we are the objects of a love we do not understand."

—Peter Kreeft

NOT GOOD ENOUGH FOR *Heaven*

A patient once told me that she felt she wasn't good enough to go to Heaven. I said, *"You're not."* Her eyes got big. I told her, *"That's why we need a Savior."* I then told her the story of the brother and sister who had gotten their school pictures. The sister complained about how poorly she looked. She said, *"These pictures don't do me justice."* Her brother responded, *"You don't want justice. You want mercy!"*—I don't know about you, but I *don't* want God's justice. I want and need God's grace, mercy, and pardon come Judgment Day. That is why the Gospel is such good news. There is mercy and forgiveness for those who don't deserve it. ❧

"CASE DISMISSED!"

The story is told of a woman who received a phone call late one night from the emergency room of a hospital stating that her dad had had a stroke. She hastily threw on some clothes and began frantically driving the 200 miles to where her father was. As she was going through one small town, she looked in her rear view mirror, and there was a police car chasing her. Because she was going so fast, the officer didn't merely give her a ticket - he arrested her. The next day she appeared before the county judge. As the judge looked over the officer's report, he said, *"Lady, what were you thinking? Do you realize you were going almost 50 miles per hour above the speed limit!? Your fine is either $300 or three days in jail."*

The young woman said, *"Oh no, your honor, you don't understand. My father is dying. I can't possibly spend three days in jail, and I'm sorry, but I left in such a hurry that I left my purse on the kitchen counter. I have no money."* The judge said, *"I'm sorry too, young lady, because the law says you must pay $300 or spend three days in jail."*

Well, the woman was crushed and she began to weep. For some reason it touched the old judge's heart. To the surprise of everyone in the court, he stood up, stepped down from the bench, walked over, took off his robe, put on his sports coat, walked around in front of the bench beside the woman, pulled out his checkbook, wrote a check for $300, and laid it on the bench. Then he put his robe back on, and resumed his seat. He said, *"Young lady, the law says you must pay $300 or spend three days in jail, but I see that someone has paid the fine for you. Case dismissed!"*

This is what God did for us. When we stood condemned, without hope, deserving hell, God took off his robe of deity, put on a robe of humanity, became a man in the person of Jesus Christ, and died to pay a fine we could never pay [Isaiah 53:4-6,11; Romans 5:6]. According to scripture, Jesus is both God and man. He has two natures: the human and the divine [Philippians 2:6,7; Romans 1:3,4.]. If we accept his offer of forgiveness, when we stand before God as Judge, we will be standing before the one who loved us and paid the fine for us: *"Case dismissed!"* (Romans 4:6,7; 8:1). ✠

Just Plain Funny

There was a man who constantly worried about anything and everything. One day the man was talking to a friend and said, "Do you know that I don't worry anymore? I've hired someone to worry for me." His friend said, "Why that's amazing. How much does it cost?" The man responded, "It's costing me $100,000 a year." "Good grief!" his friend responded. "How can you afford that?!" The man replied, "Well, that's one of the things he's worrying about."

A highway patrolman pulls an old hillbilly over and asks him if he has any I.D. The hillbilly responds, " *'bout what?*"

A man was asked what he would want to do if he only had four weeks to live. He said, "I guess I'd want to spend it with my mother-in-law." "Your mother-in-law?!!" "Yeah," he says, "It would be the four longest weeks of my life."

Coach Vince Lombardi was the infamous, tough-as-nails coach of the Green Bay Packers football team. A news reporter was interviewing one of Lombardi's football players. The reporter asked, "So, does the coach have ulcers?" The player responded, "No, he's just a carrier."

A snail got run over by a turtle and was all banged up. Another snail asked him, *"What happened to you?"* The injured snail responded, *"I'm not sure, it happened so fast."*

Bubba's truck dies and he calls to have it towed. The tow truck driver asks, "What's your address?" Bubba says, "1011 Eucalyptus Drive." The driver says, "Can you spell that for me?" There was a long silence and Bubba says, "Let me roll it over to Oak Street for you."

A nice Christian woman buys a talking parrot from a sailor. Once she got the parrot home she found that he would cuss and swear like a sailor. It was terribly embarrassing to her, so she decided that every time the parrot would cuss she'd use some behavior modification on him. The next time he cussed she took him and put him in the deep freezer for two minutes. That really got his attention and he was on good behavior for a couple of weeks, didn't say a single cuss word. Then, one day he hooked his beak on the feeder and out came a string of swear words. This time the lady took the ole' parrot and stuck him in the deep freezer for five minutes. As she was taking him out of the freezer, the parrot looked at the woman and said, "Just out of curiosity, what did that turkey in there do?"

A man kept having horrible paranoid feelings that someone was hiding under his bed. He finally went to a psychiatrist. He told the doc that he just knows there is someone hiding under his bed at night. He said that whenever he gets the courage to look under the bed he doesn't see anyone but feels the person has probably climbed on top of the bed. So, while he's never seen the person, he knows he is there. The psychiatrist says, *"This sounds like a very deep seated problem. It'll probably take some intense therapeutic sessions, at least once or twice a week for a year or two to resolve the matter."* The man said, *"How much will this cost?"* The doc says, *"$150 per session."* The man gulps and says, *"Doc, let me think about it."* A couple of weeks later the man bumps into the doc on the sidewalk and says, *"Hey, doc. Good news! I'm cured, and it only cost me $10."* The psychiatrist was stunned and asked, *"That's amazing. How is that possible?"* The man said, *"I was talking to my ole' granny about my problem and she said, 'Why don't you just cut the legs off the bed?'"*

A husband and wife were taking a trip from Nashville over to Memphis. The husband had terrible eyesight and could barely see. The wife could see fine but was almost stone deaf, so whenever they went anywhere they had to go as a pair. She was the eyes and he was the ears. As they filled up with gas at a full-service station the gas attendant was making small talk and he said, "Where ya'll from?" The husband said, "Nashville." The wife said, "What'd he say?" He said, "He just asked where we're from." She said, "Oh." The attendant said, "Nice car. What kind is it?" The husband replied, "An Old's '98." The wife said, "What'd he say?" The husband responded, "He just asked what kind of a car we have." She said, "Oh." The attendant said, "Where ya headed?" The husband said, "Memphis." The wife said, "What'd he say?" The husband said, 'He just asked where we were headed.'" She said, "Oh." Then the attendant said, "Ya know, speaking of Memphis, I knew the meanest, most cantankerous woman I ever knew who used to live in Memphis." The wife said, "What'd he say?" The husband said, "He thinks he knows your sister!"

A salesman got to thinking that he could sell a lot more Bibles if he had more sales people working for him, so he decides to run an ad in the newspaper for Bible salesmen. Three people responded. The first two were pretty normal but the third guy, he-he-he-talk-talked like this, with a real stutter. The Bible salesman said that he really appreciated the man applying but didn't think the man was really cut out to be a Bible salesman. However, the man who stuttered kept begging to be given a chance. Reluctantly the salesman agreed to give the man a chance. He sent all three sales people out to sell Bibles door-to-door. At the end of the first day the first two sales people had sold 10-15 Bibles apiece, but the third guy who stuttered had sold nearly 25 Bibles. The salesman said, "That's amazing! Let's give it one more day." The next day, the man who stuttered sold nearly 30 Bibles. The Bible salesman, in total amazement, said, "That's incredible. How are you doing it?" The man said, "Well..well..well...I...I... I..uh...uh..I go go go to to the the door and I I I ask if if they'd like like to buy buy a Bible or or if if they'd rather rather I read it to them."

Ole gets his first cell phone and Lena calls him up and says, "Ole! Ole! It just came in over da news dat der's some idiot driving down the interstate the wrong direction near to where you are." Ole says, "Na, na! Ders hundreds of 'em!"

There was a man in a mental institution, named George, so the story goes, who believed he was dead. No matter what anyone would say or do they could not convince him he was alive. One day a mental caseworker had an idea. He said, "Tell me, George, do dead men bleed?" George thought for a minute and said, "No, dead men don't bleed." The caseworker took a needle, pricked George's finger, and squeezed. A small drop of blood appeared. George's eyes grew big as he saw the blood and he said, "Well, what do you know. Dead men do bleed!" ∽

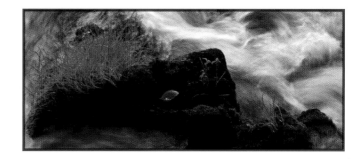

"... Nature is only the first sketch"

—C.S. Lewis from *The Weight of Glory*

These things—the beauty, the memory of our own past—are good images of what we really desire; but if they are mistaken for the thing itself, they turn into dumb idols, breaking the hearts of their worshippers. For they are not the thing itself; they are only the scent of a flower we have not found, the echo of a tune we have not heard, news from a country we have never yet visited."

—C.S. Lewis from *The Weight of Glory*

GOD IS FOR US

About 15 years ago I went through the hardest time of my entire life. Without going into the gory details, I was really hurting and my whole world was crumbling around me. Then, some strange things started happening. Every time I turned around, it seemed, the car in front of me would have a dealer's car tag.—I'd be at a stop light and the car in front of me would have a dealer's tag. I'd be nice and let someone pull in front of me and they'd have a dealer's tag on their car. This happened time after time after time. I'm not superstitious, but I began asking God whether this was coincidence, or whether He was trying to tell me something. As I prayed it seemed as though God was telling me that whenever I saw a dealer's tag it was to be a reminder that I am "dealing" with eternal issues. In other words, I was to maintain an eternal perspective on life, that the trials of this life are only temporary (II Corinthians 4:16-18).

Then another phenomenon happened. I started seeing the number 444 time after time after time. Some car would have the license plate 444. I'd wake up in the middle of the night and the digital clock would read 444. I'd glance at my digital wrist watch and it would read 444. Again I began praying, "Lord, is this coincidence or are you trying to tell me something?" As I prayed Romans 8:31 came to mind which says, "...if God is for us, who can be against us?" Since there are three Persons within the Godhead (the Father, Son, and Holy Spirit), and since they are each "4" me, 444 was to be a reminder of that truth.

On one of the very worst days of my life, I was on my way to see an attorney about a legal problem that was breaking my heart. It was a cold, drizzly, November day. I was trying to remain strong in my faith but I was fighting depression and discouragement. As I pulled onto the interstate a little white car passed me with the license plate "D-444!"

All of a sudden I felt God's peace come over me. I felt like He'd spoken to me, "Bart, keep an eternal perspective, and I want you to know that I'm for you." And He was. Against all odds things turned out OK. Years later I saw the attorney I had visited that day and he asked how things came out. When I told him he said, "Do you realize that only about one out of 100 people who go through what you did come out as well as you did?"—I thought, "Thank you, Lord, for being for (444) me."

If you are going through some trials and hard times, remember that the pains and heartaches of this life will not last forever. Do you recall the words Joseph spoke to his brothers after they sold him into slavery? Joseph said, "You meant it for evil, but God meant it for good." (Genesis 50:20) ❧

 aith comes from looking at God, not the mountain... How do you pray a prayer so filled with faith that it can move a mountain? By shifting the focus from the size of your mountain to the sufficiency of the Mountain Mover.”

—Bill Hybels

God Has Forever To Pay Back Our Losses

*S*everal years ago some good friends of mine, who live in Lincoln, Nebraska, came for a visit. They have a son named Josh. When I met Josh for the first time, he was one of the cutest, happiest kids I'd ever seen. He had bright blue eyes and a smile that would light up a room. He looked like he should have been on the cover of a children's magazine.

A few months later Josh became very ill with a temperature of 105-106 degrees. His parents took him to the emergency room. Whether the doctor was drunk, or on drugs, or just having a bad day, they don't know. The doctor was very rude and told the parents to take Josh home, give him some aspirin, and if he wasn't better to bring him back tomorrow. Rather than question the doctor, they did as they were told.

As it turns out, Josh had spinal meningitis, and because the doctor didn't catch it soon enough, Josh became 100% deaf.—My heart broke when I heard the news. I don't cry easily, but I cried. I began telling God how unfair it was, that in this lifetime Josh will never hear his parents say *"I love you."* He will never again hear the sounds of music or birds singing. I then told God, *"Lord, even if you give Josh another whole life, how could it possibly pay for all the pain and loss he will know in this life?"*

Then, it was one of those rare times in my life; I had a very real sense of God actually speaking to me. A thought, not my own, clearly came to my mind. I felt God telling me, *"Bart, I have all eternity to pay Josh back for his losses!"*

And it is true. God has forever to graciously pay back any hurts or losses we may experience in this life. If we are genuinely at peace with God when we die, knowing our sins are forgiven, it doesn't really matter what cards life has dealt us here. In the end it will be OK. ❧

POSTSCRIPT: Josh can now hear. He was killed when his car went off over a cliff while driving in the mountains.

71

on't be afraid; just believe"

"*By His grace I await death in peace, in the hope of being eternally united to Him. Yet I live with joy, whether in the prosperity which it pleases Him to bestow upon me, or in the adversity which He sends for my good . . .*"

—Pascal

"If we confess our sins, he is faithful and just and will forgive us our sins and purify us from all unrighteousness."

—1 John 1:9

"God opposes the proud but gives grace to the humble. Humble yourselves, therefore, under God's mighty hand, that he may lift you up in due time. Cast all your anxiety on him because he cares for you."

—1 Peter 5:5b-7

"We will have all eternity to explore the mysteries of God, and not just explore, but celebrate and share with one another."

— John Eldredge

"*Let us then approach the throne of grace with confidence, so that we may receive mercy and find grace to help us in our time of need.*"

—Hebrews 4:16

What Cancer Cannot Do

One of my hospice patients shared this with me.

Cancer is so limited . . .
It cannot cripple love,
It cannot shatter hope,
It cannot corrode faith,
It cannot eat away peace,
It cannot destroy confidence,
It cannot kill friendship,
It cannot silence courage,
It cannot invade the soul,
It cannot reduce eternal life,
It cannot quench the Spirit,
It cannot lessen the power of the resurrection.

If an incurable disease has invaded your life, refuse to let it touch your spirit. Your body can be severely afflicted, and you may have a great struggle. But if you keep trusting God's love, your spirit will remain strong . . . Why must I bear this pain? I cannot tell—I only know my Lord does all things well. And so I trust in God, my all in all, for He will bring me through, what'er befall.

—Smith

Our greatest enemy is not disease, but despair.

"*It is to be remembered that mountain tops are only the beginning.*"

—Brother Ramos

Catholic HUMOR

Two nurses, Catholic nuns, had gone into the country to visit a patient. On the way back to town their car ran out of gas. A passing trucker noticed the two nuns stranded along the highway so he stopped and offered to help. When he learned they were out of gas he said, "I'll gladly drain some gas from my truck and give it to you but I don't have anything to put it in." One of the nuns dug around in her car and came back with a bed pan. The trucker said, "Well, OK!" He drained some gas in the bed pan, and because he was in a hurry, he left. As the nuns were very carefully pouring the gas in the car a highway patrolman pulled up and saw what was going on. He said, "Ladies, I don't think that will work, but I sure admire your faith!"

This is a true story. For several years Campus Crusade For Christ would put together athletic teams of basketball players, wrestlers, etc. to travel around the world playing other teams and sharing their faith following each athletic event. One time the American basketball team was in Italy. They were staying in a small city and the only church in the entire town was a huge Catholic cathedral. Even though the players were not Catholic, they still wanted to attend church on Sunday, so they decided to attend this Catholic church. They arrived late and were ushered down to the very front of the church on the second row. Of course, these American basketball players, all extremely tall, stuck out like a sore thumb compared to the short Italians. To make matters worse the entire service was in either Latin or Italian and the Americans could not understand a word. The only help they got was by observing this one short Italian man on the very front row. Whenever he'd stand, they'd stand. When he sat down, they set down. One time the man stood up and they all stood up, and the congregation burst into laughter. Seeing that they were the only ones standing besides this man they all sat down very quickly. Following the service, they asked the priest, who could speak English, what had happened. He said, "We were dedicating the man's child and I asked, 'Would the father of the child please stand?'"

The pope comes to America and is picked up by a limousine chauffeur. As the pope gets in he says, "You know, I've always wanted to drive one of these. Would you mind if I drive?" Of course what could the chauffeur say, so he lets the pope drive. Going down interstate the pope is not paying attention to how fast he is driving and he flies past a highway patrolman who takes out after him and pulls him over. As soon as the pope rolls down the window and the officer sees who it is he says, "Oh my gosh! Wait here." The officer goes back to his patrol car and calls the chief of police. He says, "Chief, I've just made a horrible mistake. I've pulled over someone very important and I'm not sure what I'm supposed to do." The chief says, "Who is it? The governor?" The officer says, "No, he's more important than the governor." The chief says, "Well, is it the president?" The officer says, "No, he's even more important than the president." The chief says, "Well, who is it then?" The officer says, "I'm not sure, but the pope's his chauffeur!"

A young priest joins a monastery and takes a vow of silence. They tell him that every seven years he can say two words. At the end of the first seven years they ask him if he has anything he wants to say, and he says, "Bed hard!" They say, "All right, we'll get you a softer mattress." Another seven years goes by and they ask him if he has anything to say, and he says, "Food bad!" They say, "All right, we'll see if we can get you food that you like better." Another seven years goes by, twenty-one years later, and they ask him if he has anything to say and he says, "I quit!" The old priest responds, "No wonder. You do nothing but complain." ❧

"We know ourselves so little ..."
—Pascal

Self-Evident

"It is self-evident that the self-evident is not always self-evident."

A few years ago a little light turned on in my head when a chaplain, mentor/friend used the word *self-evident*. All of a sudden some things I'd been wrestling with in my thinking became very clear. It was as though the truth had been staring me in the face all along, but, because the answers were so common sense, so *self-evident*, I'd missed seeing them. Just as common sense is not so common these days, neither are some of the *self-evident* truths of this world. For example, it is self-evident that air surrounds us, but when was the last time you thought to yourself, *"Yep, sure enough; I'm surrounded by air and without it I'd be in big trouble!"*?

Denial and avoidance are two ways most of us deal with the thorny issues of life. We *deny* the obvious. We *avoid* talking to the doctor because we're afraid of the truth. Yet, won't you agree that we would spare ourselves a lot of pain in the long run if we would simply face the truth?

Like an ant living at the base of Mt. Everest, it is easy to get so focused on our little ant hill that we miss the bigger picture. If I may, I'd like to encourage you to lift your eyes off your current circumstances, whatever they may be, and focus on some of life's bigger *self-evident* truths which, like air, are easy to overlook. Will you think with me as I share some self-evident spiritual truths I see?

As a hospice chaplain [working with the terminally ill], and as a professional landscape photographer, I see life differently than most. I see both beauty and heartache, almost on a daily basis. And, from time to time, I see incredible faith, hope, and courage. As a photographer, I'm aware that if I can find the right matte and frame to put around a photograph, it will make the photograph look twice as pretty. The right framing enhances the beauty of the picture inside. In like manner, I believe that God has put a frame around each of our lives, and that is death. At first we hate the frame, but once we accept it, the picture inside, life itself, becomes much more precious and beautiful. Life is full of so many wonderful things if we but have eyes to see; things that are so self-evident that, just maybe, we've missed seeing them.

Self-Evident Truth #1:

God exists.

To me, one of the most obvious truths is that God exists. One night a woman brought her husband to the psychiatric hospital where I used to work. The man was as drunk as drunk could be. I asked him if he went to A.A. [Alcoholics Anonymous]. He said, *"No, I don't believe in all that God stuff."* His wife said, *"You should believe in God!"* He responded, *"I don't believe there is a God."*—At that point I couldn't resist, so I said, *"I think there is an easy way to prove to you there is a God."* He took the bait, so I said, *"See that picture behind you? Would you believe me if I said there was an explosion at a paint factory and it blew paint everywhere and just by chance made that painting?"* He said, *"No."* I asked, *"Why not?"* He said, *"It couldn't happen."*—I responded, *"So, whenever you see design, there is usually a designer, or when you see art, there is usually an artist, right?"* He said, *"Yeah."* Then I said, *"When you look at Cindy Crawford, the supermodel, or an Arabian stallion, a rose, a New England Fall, or a butterfly, do they look like something the universe puked out by accident, or does it look like there's design?"* He said, *"Design."*—I said, *"Then there must be a Designer, and that is God."* He said, *"##**#, you got me!"*

Self-Evident Truth #2:

God is awesome beyond belief.

It doesn't take a rocket scientist to figure out that if God exists, then God is awesome beyond belief. By merely looking up at the night sky, and gazing at the stars, that isn't hard to see.

For example, the largest star we can see with the naked eye is a star located in the southern sky, during the winter months, in the constellation Orion. The name of the star is Betelgeuse [pronounced *beetle juice*]. It is the upper left reddish star just above Orion's belt of three stars. Betelgeuse is so big that approximately 160 million of our suns would fit inside it. It has a diameter of approximately 250 million miles. If our earth were the size of a golf ball, by comparison, Betelgeuse would be a ball 2 miles high. If there were a tunnel through the center of that star, driving at 55 miles per hour, it would take us 1,600 years just to drive through the tunnel. [It would only take 193 years to drive from here to our sun.] If Betelgeuse was sitting where our sun is, the orbits of Mercury, Venus, Earth, Mars, and Jupiter would all be inside it.

To put the size of our universe in perspective, *National Geographic* [May 1974, p. 592] had this to say: *"Imagine that the thickness of this page represents the distance from earth to the sun [93,000,000 miles, or about eight light-minutes]. Then the distance to the nearest star [4 1/3 light years] is a 71-foot-high sheaf of paper. And the diameter of our own galaxy [100,000 light-years] is a 310-mile stack, while the edge of the known universe is not reached until the pile of paper is 31 million miles high—a third of the way to the sun!"*

If the universe is incredible, then the God who created it is even more incredible.

Self-Evident Truth #3:

We live in a little speck of time suspended between two eternities.

*I*magine a piece of chalk the size of a telephone pole [50-60 feet tall], and a chalkboard hundreds of miles long. Pretend you take that huge piece of chalk and draw a thin line that goes and goes until the chalk runs out. Think of this as a time line representing eternity, except that with eternity the chalk never runs out. Now, put a tiny dot at the front end of that line, and let it represent your whole life here on earth compared to eternity.

First, does it matter whether God exists?—Of course. If there is no God, you might as well erase the line, for when you die the party is over—forever! In which case, you should drink all the enjoyment you can out of this tiny dot of time, for that is all you will ever get.

On the other hand, if God is real, and there is an afterlife, then nothing on earth could be more important. You are literally at the beginning of forever; be it good, bad, or otherwise. Things such as war, a terminal illness, making money, marriage, having kids, national freedom, getting an education—even sex—would not begin to compare in importance to that which will affect you eternally.

Latest statistics say that 100% of every generation will die. We are each living one breath and one heartbeat away from eternity. Pascal, the French mathematician who devised the formulas for probability and chance, and was a forerunner of calculus, said it was amazing to him that people worry and fritter over temporal things which are of no eternal consequence, while at the same time living without forethought or seeming concern for that which will affect them throughout eternity.

We are eternal spiritual beings. Only that which is spiritual is of eternal lasting value.

I once read a book by Bruce Larson where he commented that the Bible is not primarily a book of theology, although it contains a lot of theology. He said the Bible is not primarily a book of history or prophecy, although it obviously contains a lot of history and prophecy. As I read, to be honest, I began to wonder, *"What's left?"* He then pointed out that the Bible is primarily a book of relationships: one's relationship with God, with one's neighbor, and with oneself, and that if we miss the *relational*, we have missed what life and the Bible are all about.

Speaking candidly, as a hospice chaplain, the greatest sadness I feel in working with terminally ill patients is *not* the death of the patient. It is seeing the tragedy of wasted lives; of witnessing the devastating consequences brought about by the bad choices some people have made throughout their lives as they have pursued their own self interests apart from God. It tears my heart out when I listen to people like the man I spoke with earlier today who wept as he lamented the many "wasted years" of his life, when he could have known God, but, out of rebellion, had chosen to bully his way through life with disastrous results. He had a failed marriage, and now had terminal throat cancer because of years of smoking or chewing tobacco. Thankfully, he made his peace with God a few years ago, but he cannot bring back the many wasted years. Others waste a whole lifetime.

It saddens me when I see patients who not only don't understand the spiritual, they haven't a clue. Some of them don't even know that they don't know. They are spiritually in the dark with no hunger for God. With only days or weeks to live, they will soon be taking life's final exam before Almighty God, and they come with empty hands, empty hearts, and empty lives–totally unprepared. They somehow hope that God will grade on the curve and not hold them accountable for their foolish choices and their stubborn self-will.

The good news for some of them, and the most redeeming part about my job, is that I can tell them that it is never too late to make peace with God. There is still hope. According to scripture, while God doesn't grade on the curve, Jesus took the test for them [and for you and me]. If they will humble themselves, and ask for God's forgiveness, which is free for all who will place their faith in Christ [John 1:12;3:16, I John 5:11-13, Ephesians 2:8,9], then Jesus will trade His test scores for theirs. Instead of flunking, God will mark down a perfect score [Romans 4:7,8].—God's grace and mercy in accepting such people still amazes me.

I was visiting with a patient, an old hillbilly-sort of fellow who lived in an old farm house back in the Ozark hills. He'd not been to church in over seventy years. I asked him,

"John [not his real name], *this is a big question, but how are you doing spiritually? Do you feel at peace with God?"* He responded, *"No, I think I'm going to that other place* [hell]." I then asked him if he'd heard the story Jesus told about the prodigal son [Luke 15]. He said, *"No."*

So, I proceeded to tell him the story of the young man who took his share of his father's inheritance and left home at an early age, where he proceeded to waste all his money on wild living: wine, women, and song. Then, Jesus said, a famine hit the land and before long the young lad hit bottom. Mustering his courage, he decided to return to his father, like a dog with its tail between its legs, totally whipped. The Bible says that while the young man was still a ways from home, the father [representing God] saw him, ran to him, hugged and kissed him, put a ring on his finger, a robe on his back, killed the fatted calf, and threw a party.

I told John, *"Do you know that, to my knowledge, the only time the image is ever used of God running in the Bible, is when He ran to that son, hugged him, and welcomed him home?"* Then I said, *"John, if you want to know how God feels about you, that's it. It is never too late. Better late than never."* Then I asked, *"John, are you ready to come home? Are you willing to come back to God?"* He thought it over and finally said, *"Yes."*—I then shared a prayer of commitment with him and invited him to pray along with me, which he did. Two days later he died. I fully expect to see him when I get to Heaven.

The prayer I shared with him went something like this: *"Dear Lord Jesus, I thank You for loving me. I am sorry for the sin, and pride, and lack of trust that has kept me from You. I believe You died on the cross and rose again to pay for my sin which has separated me from You. As best as I know how, right now, I place my life in Your hands. I invite You to come into my life. Forgive me of my sin and make me the person You want me to be. Calm my fears, carry my burdens, and open my heart to receive Your love. Thank You for hearing this prayer. Amen."*

By now it should be *self-evident* to you that eternal issues are at stake [for all of us]. If, for whatever reason, you have never seriously considered entering into a relationship with God, or, through denial or avoidance, you have blocked God and eternal issues out of your mind, may I encourage you to please reconsider. The God I know is not only awesomely powerful and holy, the Creator and Judge before whom you will one day stand, God is also a God of love, mercy, and forgiveness who invites you to come to his *party*—which will last for all eternity. C.S. Lewis states, and I totally agree, *"Joy is the serious business of Heaven."* Oh the joy that awaits those who know and love God.

Jesus said, *"Whoever comes to me I will never drive away."* [John 6:37] The question is *"Will you come?"*—There is no single question of greater importance that you will ever have to answer in this lifetime. You've received God's invitation. What will your response be? ∞

"He has made everything beautiful in its time. He has also set eternity in the hearts of men."

—Ecclesiastes 3:11a

"*I* announce to you redemption. Behold I make all things new. Behold I do what cannot be done. I restore the years that the locusts and worms have eaten. I restore the years which you have drooped away upon your crutches and in your wheel-chair. I restore the symphonies and operas which your deaf ears have never heard . . . I bring you the Love of which all other loves speak, the Love which is joy and beauty, and which you have sought in a thousand streets and for which you have wept and clawed your pillow."

—Thomas Howard from *Christ the Tiger*

"*Her* absence is like the sky, spread over everything."

C. S. Lewis from *A Grief Observed*, as he writes of his wife's death

"*In this you greatly rejoice, though now for a little while you may have had to suffer grief in all kinds of trials. These have come so that your faith—of greater worth than gold, which perishes even though refined by fire—may be proved genuine and may result in praise, glory and honor when Jesus Christ is revealed.*"

—1 Peter 1:6-7

"*Some people tell me they don't need to schedule regular time for prayer; they pray on the run. These people are kidding themselves. Just try building a marriage on the run. To get to know someone, you have to slow down and spend time together.*"

—Bill Hybels from *Too Busy Not to Pray*

"*But as for me, it is good to be near God.*"

—Psalm 73:28a

"For you created my inmost being; you knit me together in my mother's womb. I praise you because I am fearfully and wonderfully made; your works are wonderful, I know that full well. My frame was not hidden from you when I was made in the secret place. When I was woven together in the depths of the earth, your eyes saw my unformed body. All the days ordained for me were written in your book before one of them came to be. How precious to me are your thoughts, O God! How vast is the sum of them! Were I to count them, they would outnumber the grains of sand. When I awake, I am still with you."

—Psalm 139:13-18

A Wedding

I once performed a wedding for a young couple. The wedding was held on a river barge which had been converted into a floating restaurant on the Missouri River. It was a beautiful setting. Looking outside the windows we could see the massive Missouri River flowing past the restaurant windows. As I tried to emphasize how short and how precious life is, and for them not to forget it, I had them look at the river. I said, "Pretend this is a river of time, sort of like eternity flowing past us. Now, imagine picking up a tiny grain of sand and throwing it into the river." I told them that their whole life on earth was like that little grain of sand, that all eternity was before them, and that what truly mattered in life was knowing and loving God. ⌘

Heaven

"In speaking of this desire for our own far-off country, which we find in ourselves even now, I feel a certain shyness. I am almost committing an indecency. I am trying to rip open the inconsolable secret in each one of you—the secret which hurts so much that you take your revenge on it by calling it names like Nostalgia and Romanticism and Adolescence . . . [it is] the secret we cannot hide and cannot tell, though we desire to do both. We cannot tell it because it is a desire for something that has never actually appeared in our experience. We cannot hide it because our experience is constantly suggesting it, and we betray ourselves like lovers at the mention of a name."

—C.S. Lewis from *The Weight of Glory*

I recall my heart aching as I read this quote. It helped me realize that the pain I'd lived with all my life could be good if it directed my heart toward Heaven. It also gave me hope that the pain would not last forever.

"There is no fear in love. But perfect love drives out fear, because fear has to do with punishment. The one who fears is not made perfect in love."

—I John 4:18

"Heaven offers more than comfort; it offers compensation."

—Randy Alcorn from the book, *Heaven*

CAN I PRAY & EXPECT GOD TO HEAL ME?

As a chaplain, I would like to address three questions which trouble many patients who are facing terminal or life-threatening illnesses. I by no means have the last word on this, but hopefully these thoughts will help.

Question #1: "Is God punishing me because I'm sick?"

Think with me. In many ways, the question of whether cancer, or any life-threatening illness, is a form of God's judgment or punishment is irrelevant. According to scripture, *all* of us are under judgment for our sins until those sins are forgiven (Romans 3:9-26; 6:23; Ephesians 2:1-9). The good news is that God loves you, and Christ died for your sins so that you could escape the just judgment of God (John 3:16-18). Once you are forgiven, whether you are physically healed or not, you are no longer under God's eternal judgment or condemnation. Romans 8:1 says, *"Therefore, there is now no condemnation for those who are in Christ Jesus."* Romans 4:7-8 says, *"Blessed are they whose transgressions are forgiven, whose sins are covered. Blessed is the man* (woman) *whose sin the Lord will never count against him."*—Now that is good news. Until God establishes his Kingdom on this earth, death and sickness will remain part of life. *All* of us will die. It is only a matter of when. I don't want to minimize what you are going through, but in the bigger scheme of things, how you or I die is really of little consequence. Where we spend eternity is everything.

Speaking candidly, sometimes physical illness *may* be a sign of God's discipline. According to Paul one reason many Christians in Corinth were sick, and some had even died, was because they partook of the Lord's Supper in an unholy manner (I Corinthians 11:27-30). Jesus once told an invalid man whom He had healed, *"Stop sinning or something worse may happen to you."* (John 5:14b). If you're living in known sin, you may want to ask God to forgive you and for him to give you the power to stop.

On the other hand, sometimes illness has nothing to do with sin, and may in fact be a way in which God chooses to be glorified. Do you recall the story of the man born blind and how Jesus' disciples asked whether this man or his parents had sinned? He said, *"Neither this man nor his parents sinned. . .but this happened so that the work of God might be displayed in his life."* (John 9:1-3). As a chaplain, I am so moved when those who are dying choose to trust God in spite of their suffering. Job said, *"Though he slay me, yet will I hope in him."* (Job 13:15).—Now that is faith!

Lastly, sometimes our illnesses are our own doing. We all recognize the fact that we bring on some sickness by our choices: smoking, not exercising, worrying, eating junk food, doing drugs, etc.—Is God to blame for this?—No, no more than I blaming God if the engine on my car blows because I never change the oil. Some illnesses are the natural consequences of the choices we make.

Question #2. "But what about the illnesses that are not my fault? God obviously allows them."

Yes he does. The question is, *"Why?"* Please think with me: people who ask these questions are in essence asking, "Is God unjust? Is God really good?"—Once we state it that way, most of us see how ridiculous those underlying assumptions and doubts are. If God is not good and loving we're all in *big* trouble! However, based on God's character as revealed in scripture we know that God is holy, loving and good. Correct? God can do no wrong. If you and I could trade places with God, and see as God sees, and know as God knows, do you realize that we would not change a single thing that God is currently doing? Why? Because it would all make sense. God has His reasons for everything.

We get ourselves into trouble when we try to second guess God. Our perspective on life is so limited. God sees the bigger picture. We don't. When we get to Heaven it will either all make sense, or it won't matter, for we will know that God was right in allowing/causing what He did. Often the things in life which are the very worst for us physically turn out to be the very best for us spiritually. As a chaplain I see this time and time again. The physical is temporal. The spiritual is eternal. Weigh them out and the eternal will win every time. (See II Corinthians 4:16-18). Therefore, whatever reason(s) God has for allowing suffering, it comes from a heart of love and goodness (Psalm 73:21-26). Even His judgments are a form of His mercy.

According to the creation account in Genesis: sin, sickness and pain were *not* part of God's original plan. They came as the result of man's sin and rebellion. God is just when he punishes. God honored Adam and Eve by giving them free will, but warned them of the consequences; that death would result if they disobeyed and ate the forbidden fruit. Sickness and death are a constant warning to us of the seriousness of sin, as well as a sober reminder that there are consequences for our behavior. God takes our choices seriously. We should too. Apart from God's grace, what we sow, we will likely reap.

Read the Old Testament and you will see that God's judgments and punishment of Israel, though severe, were meant to bring the nation back to God. The book of Hosea is a classic. More than any other Old Testament book it catalogs the sins of Israel, and yet it most clearly shows God's love for His people. God hated executing judgment on Israel. It broke His heart [Hosea 11:8, 9]. He gave them warning after warning until there was no choice left but to judge. C.S. Lewis rightly says that pain is like a megaphone [amplifier] that God uses to awaken a deafened world.—And it works! Pain definitely gets our attention. It will either drive us closer to God or further away. God always means it for good.

Let me tell you about leprosy. Leprosy is a disease of the nerves. People with leprosy lose the ability to feel. It is not, as I used to think, some horrible disease which eats away the flesh. The reason lepers' hands and feet seem to rot away is because they lose feeling and keep hurting themselves, over and over again, until irreversible damage has been done. Fingers and toes wear away.

Did you know that in studies with lepers, the *only* thing that prevented them from hurting themselves was pain? Some doctors, in trying to help leprosy patients, hooked up some artificial warning devices to let lepers know when they were hurting themselves. They devised bells, buzzers and flashing lights. The lepers would turn them off and do whatever they were going to do anyway. Why? Because

it didn't hurt. Pain [an electrical shock] was the *only* thing doctors found that kept lepers from hurting themselves.

Without pain we'd be like those lepers. It's a sad fact, but true. *We need pain* in order to keep from hurting ourselves—physically, spiritually, and emotionally. Please read Romans 8:18-25. Paul says that God both allows, and even causes, pain and frustrations to produce a *hope* and a longing for heaven. Paul says that God is the one who subjected the creation to frustration. —That is a hard pill to swallow. You mean God is responsible for some of the pain and frustrations we experience?—Yes. For example, who longs for Heaven the most: a person going through suffering, or someone living the "good life" with fancy cars and a mansion? God doesn't want us to get confused about where our real home is. Our home is in heaven. Pain and trials bring that lesson home loud and clear.—God is often nearest to us in our pain.

Suffering also helps us identify with the sufferings of Christ. We begin to appreciate what Jesus went through for us on the cross. When we suffer we also discover God's comfort, which in turn helps us comfort others who are hurting. (Please read II Corinthians 1:3-11.)

Question #3: "Can I pray *&* expect God to heal me?"

Yes, you may pray. Sometimes God will answer yes, sometimes no. But, rest assured, God will do what is right. The main thing to remember is that you are truly loved by him. It is within God's power to heal you. And, in some cases he may. I know people who have been miraculously healed. I encourage you to humbly ask God to heal you. Ask him to do what is *best* for you and those you love. Pray that God will do that which most glorifies him. Sometimes God will take us out of the storm. Other times he takes the storm away from us. But more often than not God walks *through* the storm with us. Remember, 100% of us will die sometime.—Even men and women of faith eventually die.

Let me also encourage you *not* to equate being healed, or not being healed, with how much God loves you and can use you. Scripturally, God is far more concerned about your spiritual well-being than your body (although both are important).

What is most important to God are things such as faith, walking in love, humility, being grateful, etc. If your heart is right with God, it's going to be OK. Relax and trust God. If physical well-being were a sign of spiritual maturity, then anyone with a physical ailment or handicap would be a second-class Christian. That is simply not what scripture teaches. Some of God's greatest saints have had handicaps. Fanny Crosby, whose hymns have touched millions, was blind. The apostle Paul most likely had severe eye problems (II Corinthians 12:1-10; Galatians 6:11). Not all illness is linked to sin or unforgiveness. (See: II Corinthians 12:7-10; John 9:2-3; I Timothy 5:23; II Timothy 4:20).

If you are ill and possibly facing death, while I do not know whether God will heal you or not, God will do what is best. Think with me. Do you believe God loves you?—The answer is, "Yes." (John 3:16; Romans 5:8). God loves you with a perfect love. Secondly, is God all powerful? "Yes."—Now, put these two concepts together. God unconditionally loves you and He is all powerful. What this means is that all of the love, and all of the power behind the whole universe, is focused on loving you to the degree that you are able to receive it, and in the way that is best for you.—That is absolutely amazing. Think about it. This thought can revolutionize the way you think about God.

If you have given God control of your life, then your life and your body are no longer yours, but his [Romans 12:1,2; I Corinthians 6:20]. Paul wrote in Philippians 1:20b-21, *"so . . . now as always Christ will be exalted in my body, whether by life or by death. For to me, to live is Christ and to die is gain."*—For the believer, death is not a thing to dread (Hebrews 2:14,15), but is rather our ticket home, into the arms of the One who loves us and died for us (Psalm 116:15; Acts 7:55-59). If we know Christ we are in a win-win situation. "To live is Christ and to die is gain". My suggestion?—Quit worrying about your illness, and stop second-guessing God. Pray about it, and then leave the outcome to him. ✥

*J*esus said, "Whoever comes to me I will never drive away."

—John 6:37b

Will We Know Each Other In Heaven?

As a hospice chaplain, this is one of my most frequently asked questions. I think the answer is, "Yes."—First, we are all brothers and sisters in Christ, one church. We will all be "one." (John 17:20,21). We will live together (John 14:1,2; Revelation 21). We will see each other at the judgment (Luke 12:2,3; I Corinthians 6:2,3). In the Bible those who have died still retain their identity. Moses is still Moses. Abraham is still Abraham (e.g., Luke 16:19-31). David looked forward to seeing his deceased son (II Samuel 12:23). Nowhere in scripture does it say we won't know each other. Common sense says we will know and love one another for all eternity. ❧

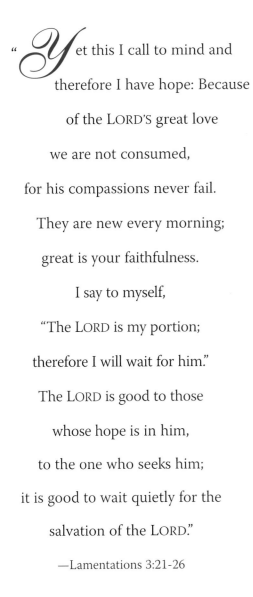

"Yet this I call to mind and
therefore I have hope: Because
of the LORD'S great love
we are not consumed,
for his compassions never fail.
They are new every morning;
great is your faithfulness.
I say to myself,
"The LORD is my portion;
therefore I will wait for him."
The LORD is good to those
whose hope is in him,
to the one who seeks him;
it is good to wait quietly for the
salvation of the LORD."

—Lamentations 3:21-26

A Thought to Ponder

*W*hy is God landing in this enemy-occupied world in disguise and starting a sort of secret society to undermine the devil? Why is He not landing in force, invading it? . . . I wonder whether people who ask God to interfere openly and directly in our world quite realize what it will be like when He does. When that happens, it is the end of the world. When the author walks on to the stage the play is over. God is going to invade, all right: but what is the good of saying you are on His side then, when you see the whole natural universe melting away like a dream and something else—something it never entered your head to conceive—comes crashing in; something so beautiful to some of us and so terrible to others that none of us will have any choice left? For this time it will be God without disguise; something so overwhelming that it will strike either irresistible love or irresistible horror into every creature. It will be too late then to choose your side. There is no use saying you choose to lie down when it has become impossible to stand up . . . Now, today, this moment, is our chance to choose the right side. God is holding back to give us that chance. It will not last forever. We must take it or leave it." ☙

—C.S. Lewis from *Mere Christianity*

Footprints In The Sand

One night a man had a dream. He dreamed he
was walking along the beach with the Lord.
Across the sky flashed scenes from his life. For each scene,
he noticed two sets of footprints in the sand:
one belonging to him, and the other to the Lord.
When the last scene of his life flashed before him,
he looked back at the footprints in the sand.
He noticed that many times along the path of his life
there was only one set of footprints.
He also noticed that it happened at the very lowest
and saddest times in his life. This really bothered him
and he questioned the Lord about it:
"Lord, you said that once I decided to follow you,
you'd walk with me all the way.
But I have noticed that during the most troublesome times
in my life there is only one set of footprints.
I don't understand why, when I needed you most,
you would leave me."
The Lord replied, *"My precious, precious child,*
I love you and I would never leave you.
During your times of trial and suffering,
when you see only one set of footprints in the sand,
it was then that I carried you."

—Mary Stevenson

"*What is the chief end of man? To know God and enjoy Him forever*"

—John Calvin

When *Life* Seems Unjust

The Psalmist, in Psalm 73, complained to God that life is not fair. He told God that evil people prosper, while good people suffer and die young. It's just not fair! He said the whole matter was perplexing to him *until* he considered the end of life and the judgment to come. He realized that God's justice would win out in the end. It is like Paul wrote, "Do not be deceived.: God cannot be mocked. A man reaps what he sows." (Galatians 6:7) Listen to the Psalmist's conclusion:

"When my heart was grieved
and my spirit embittered,
I was senseless and ignorant;
I was a brute beast before you.
Yet I am always with you;
you hold me by my right hand.
You guide me with your counsel,
and afterward you will
take me into glory.
Whom have I in heaven but you?
And earth has nothing
I desire besides you.
My flesh and my heart may fail,
but God is the strength of my heart
and my portion forever."

—Psalm 73:21-26

Answering The 'Why' Questions

One of the hardest questions I am ever asked as a chaplain is

"Why...?"—

> *"Why did I get cancer?"*

> *"Why did my daughter die?"*

> *"Why did God allow the Trade Center in New York to be bombed?"*

I'm not God, nor do I presume to speak for God, but may I offer a few reflections I hope you will find helpful.

1. God is still in control. God has not hit the panic button. Lean back and leave the driving to God. If God is your copilot, switch seats.

2. C.S. Lewis once wrote that *"Pain is a megaphone which God uses to awaken a deafened world."*—Whether we like it or not, when it comes to war, disease, or pain of any kind, it definitely gets our attention. It is like the old farmer who had the most stubborn mule in the county. No one was able to break him, so, rather than getting rid of him, the farmer hired a big city mule trainer with the reputation of being able to tame any animal. When the mule trainer arrived he walked out into the barn lot, picked up a two-by-four board, went over to the mule, reared back, and hit the mule right between the eyes. The mule fell to the ground and got back up shaking its head. The concerned farmer ran out and said, *"Why did you do that?!!"* The mule trainer replied, *"I had to get his attention first."*—Have you noticed how much spiritual awareness has come as a result of the terrorist attacks? Though God is not the author of evil, God can certainly use it to get our attention.

3. When it comes to war or terrorism, we often mistakenly think that they increase death. Not so. They merely speed up the process a bit. 100% of every generation still dies [latest statistics]. The real issue of life is not that we die, but rather the fact that each of us lives one breath and one heartbeat from eternity. War, terrorism, pandemics, or terminal illnesses simply bring to our consciousness conditions which have existed ever since Adam and Eve, namely death.

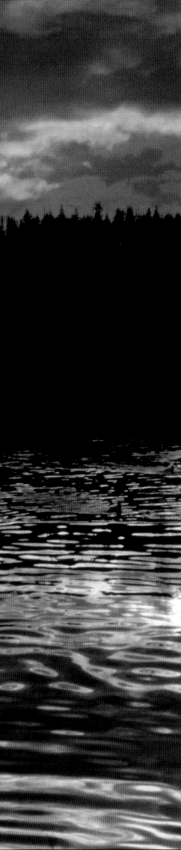

4. Would you rather know death is coming and have time to prepare, or would you rather die suddenly without warning at the hand of some terrorist? I dare say there was not a single person who walked into the Trade Center in New York on September 11, 2001 thinking, *"This is the last day of my life."* I used to think that when it came time for me to die that I wanted death to come suddenly. *"Lord, let me have a heart attack or get run over by a Mack Truck; just get it over with!"*—I no longer feel that way. Having been a hospice chaplain, I've seen how many wonderful things can happen when a person has time to prepare for death. There is time to say goodbye, to heal wounded relationships, to seek divine forgiveness, and put one's house in order.

For example, what if a woman became pregnant on Monday and had the baby on Tuesday. Would she be ready?—No. But, if she has nine months to prepare, when the baby comes she is as ready as she can be. Obviously, there are some negative aspects to a slower death, but from where I sit, when I weigh them out, under most circumstances I would choose a slower death. You've witnessed the grief on television of people who never got to tell their loved ones goodbye.Would you prefer to be in their shoes, or have extended time to spend with your loved ones?

5. Question: Do you love your car? Does your car love you? No. You may like your car, but true love cannot exist between man and machine. God created us as choice-makers, with free wills so that we would not be like a car or some robot. God desires our voluntary love.

What if I told you, *"I'll take you out for lunch, and you can have whatever you want. You can have pizza, pizza, or pizza. What do you want?"*—That is no choice. God, in like manner, could have said, *"You have a choice. You can love me . . . or you can love me . . . or you can love me."*—Again, that is no choice. For real love and goodness to exist between us and God, without us being mere robots, there had to be an alternative, a real choice: evil. As much as we hate it, that is the price tag for having freedom of choice.—We can love God or hate God. We can choose to love people, or we can crash an airplane into the building where they work. We have the potential to do great good or great evil. Why? Because love demands a choice and God gives us that choice.

6. While we have free will, a major theme in virtually every major religion is that someday there will be a day of judgment. While we have freedom of choice, there are consequences for the choices we make. We are accountable. That which we do in this life will echo for eternity.

7. The good news, from a Christian perspective, is that God is not immune to our pain, but rather entered our world, died for our sins, and is able to meet us in our pain. The message of the cross is that not only did Christ die for our sins, but that He meets and identifies with us in our pain, in the ways we've been sinned against. God comforts us as one who has known pain and injustice.

8. God has all eternity to graciously pay us back for the hurts and losses we know in this life [Romans 8:18-25].

9. Quoting C.S. Lewis again, *"When the author walks on to the stage the play is over."* God will not allow suffering and evil to go unchecked forever. There is a day coming when God will say, *"Enough's enough!"* God is a God of justice. Evil will be judged, and every tear will be wiped away from our eyes. [Revelation 21:4]

10. Until that day, since none of us know when our day will come, it is both necessary and fitting that we be ready. We all live on the threshold of eternity. God offers comfort now, and eternal hope for the future. There is unconditional forgiveness and pardon for all who place their trust in Him [John 1:12, 3:16; Ephesians 2:8,9; I John 1:9]. In the end, for those who have chosen to place their faith and trust in God, it will be *"OK!"* Good will prevail. God will reign triumphant, goodness will be rewarded, and evil will be remembered no more. ❧

"We have a homing instinct . . . and it doesn't ring for earth."
—Peter Kreeft

Stepping Through
The Door

The story is told about a man who took a trip to London, England. His tour group made a stop at Westminster Cathedral. The bus parked in the back parking lot and as they were entering through one of the back entrances he had to use the restroom. He quietly slipped away from the group. When he came out of the restroom, the whole tour group had moved on and he was lost. As he was wandering the back hallways of Westminster Cathedral, trying to figure out where his group had gone, he noticed a small hallway with a door at the end of it. For some reason he thought, "Just maybe they went through there."

As it turns out, that door was one of the side entrances into the cathedral itself. As he stepped through that door he was not in the least prepared for what he saw: the massive pillars and the glorious architecture. The sun was pouring through the stained glass windows and, as it so happened, the choir was there for choir practice. He had no more than stepped through the door when they burst into song. Between the beauty and the music, he just broke down and cried.

That is how I think it will be when we die. We will go down that narrow corridor at the end of this life and as we step through that small door at the end, we will come into something so gloriously beautiful that we too may well break down and weep tears of joy. No cost or sacrifice will have been too great. Not to be able to pass through that door would be to miss life itself. ♋

"*I shall pass through this world but once. If, therefore, there be any kindness I can show, or any good thing I can do, let me do it now, let me not defer it or neglect it, for I shall not pass this way again.*"

—Etienne De Grellet

"We are told to deny ourselves and to take up our crosses in order that we may follow Christ; and nearly every description of what we shall ultimately find if we do so contains an appeal to desire. . . Indeed, if we consider the unblushing promises of reward and the staggering nature of the rewards promised in the Gospels, it would seem that Our Lord finds our desires not too strong, but too weak. We are half-hearted creatures, fooling about with drink and sex and ambition when infinite joy is offered us." ∝

—C.S. Lewis from *The Weight of Glory*, my all-time favorite book

"*There is no joy like the joy of reunion, because there is no sorrow like the sorrow of separation.*"

—John Eldredge

" *By faith we know His existence; in glory we shall know His nature.*"

—Pascal

"'Two things pierce the human heart,' wrote Simone Weil. 'One is beauty. The other is affliction.'"

—John Eldredge

Share Your *Faith* With Me

*S*everal years ago I went through a few years of horribly difficult trials (financial, legal, marital, work, etc.). I was deeply in debt from two failed business ventures. Both failed because of circumstances out of my control. My wife was having to take about three months off from work without pay. I was behind on my house payments. I was on the verge of bankruptcy. It was December 3rd, and as I walked into my place of employment, my boss had tears in his eyes. He said, *"Bart, you've just been laid off!"*

It could not have come at a worse time. For two or three days I stewed, and worried, and fretted. I was worried about keeping a roof over our heads, let alone have any sort of Christmas for our girls. My wife and I hadn't purchased a single Christmas present.

About the third day I asked the Lord to forgive me for not trusting that He would provide for me. I told the Lord, *"Lord, I want to have faith that you'll provide, but I just can't muster the faith. I want to believe you, but I don't have it in me."* Then I prayed something I'd never prayed before. I prayed, *"Lord Jesus, I want to trust you that you'll provide for me, but I don't have it. Would you share your faith with me?"*

Within 15 minutes I received a phone call from one of the larger restaurants in town, and they ordered $3,500 worth of my photographs. Then, a couple of days later I received a check for $1,000, a gift from a friend. Then, a day or so later, I received another check for $500. Then I found out that I was getting some severance pay, and another hospital offered me a job. God provided. We had a modest but wonderful Christmas. I didn't have to declare bankruptcy. While it took me many more years to pay off all my debts, I still look back on that time of trial and I think of Jesus' faithfulness in sharing his faith with me when I had none of my own. ❧

"Forgiveness is setting the prisoner free, only to find out that the prisoner was me."

—Corrie Ten Boom

111

"To desire something and not to have it—is this not the source of nearly all our pain and sorrow?"

—John Eldredge

"There have been times
when I think we do not desire
Heaven; but more often I find
myself wondering whether,
in our heart of hearts, we
have ever desired anything else."

—C.S. Lewis from *The Problem of Pain*

"Why set any limits on God's
generosity or imagination?
Whatever the truth about Heaven,
it will be more, not less,
that these speculations; more
than our wildest dreams."

—Peter Kreeft from *Everything You Ever
Wanted To Know About Heaven*

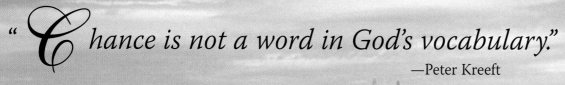

"*Chance is not a word in God's vocabulary.*"
—Peter Kreeft

A Picture of Salvation

from *"The Silver Chair"* by C.S. Lewis

"Will you promise not to—do anything to me, if I do come?" said Jill. "I make no promise," said the Lion... "Do you eat girls?" she said. "I have swallowed up girls and boys, women and men, kings and emperors, cities and realms," said the Lion. It didn't say this as if it were boasting, nor as if it were sorry, nor as if it were angry. It just said it. "I daren't come and drink," said Jill. "Then you will die of thirst," said the Lion. "Oh dear!" said Jill, coming another step nearer. "I suppose I must go and look for another stream then." "There is no other stream," said the Lion."

AUTHOR'S NOTE: The Silver Chair is one of seven books in C.S. Lewis' Chronicles of Narnia. Narnia is a land where Christ appears as a powerful lion named Aslan. Jill makes the discovery that when we come to Aslan [Christ] we come on his terms. It is a beautiful picture of salvation. In the book, once she drinks, they end up embracing.

"*eep within every person is a longing to be connected to a story larger than ourselves*
...to a dream that is bigger than we are."

—Tom Sine

"The only ultimate disaster that can

befall us, I have come to realize,

is to feel ourselves to be at home here on earth.

As long as we are aliens,

we cannot forget our true homeland."

—Malcom Muggeridge

"The great thing to remember

is that, though our feelings come and go,

His love for us does not."

— C. S. Lewis

"Most people live unprepared

for death... God uses suffering

and impending death to unfasten us

from this earth and to set our minds

on what lies beyond."

—Randy Alcorn from the book, *Heaven*

"*Worry is God's invitation to pray.*"
—Jerry Rouse

"There are only two kinds of people in the end: those who say to God, 'Thy will be done' and those to whom God says, in the end, '*Thy* will be done.' All that are in Hell, choose it. Without that self-choice there could be no Hell. No soul that seriously and constantly desires joy will ever miss it. Those who seek find. To those who knock it is opened."

—C.S. Lewis from *The Great Divorce*

"If anyone would come after me, he must deny himself and take up his cross and follow me. For whoever wants to save his life will lose it, but whoever loses his life for me will find it."

—Matthew 16:24,25

" *I pity the man who never thinks about heaven.*"

—J.C. Ryle

"*The true story of each person is the journey of his or her heart.*"

—John Eldredge

"*The rain came down, the streams rose, and the winds blew and beat against that house; yet it did not fall, because it had its foundation on the rock.*"

—Jesus, Matthew 7:25

"The God who loved you and me
enough to die for us is not
going to play games with our lives."

—Paul Little

"For I am convinced that neither
death nor life, neither angels
nor demons, neither the present
nor the future, nor any powers,
neither height nor depth, nor anything
else in all creation, will be able to
separate us from the love of God that
is in Christ Jesus our Lord."

—Romans 8:38,39

"*The utopian mindset . . . generally includes everything imaginable—shopping centers, recreation facilities, educational and artistic institutions. Only one thing is never part of the plan: a cemetery.*"

—Gerard Reed

124

"*J*esus declared, 'I tell you the truth,

no one can see the kingdom of God

unless he is born again'...

For God so loved the world that

he gave his one and only Son,

that whoever believes in him

shall not perish but have eternal life.

For God did not send his Son into the

world to condemn the world,

but to save the world through him.

Whoever believes in him is not

condemned, but whoever does not believe

stands condemned already because

he has not believed in the name of

God's one and only Son."

—John 3:3, 16-18

Who Is This Man

"A man who was merely a man and said
the sort of things Jesus said would not be
a great moral teacher.
He would either be a lunatic
—on a level with the man who says he is
a poached egg–or else he would be
the Devil of Hell.
You must make your choice.
Either this man was,
and is, the Son of God;
or else a madman or something worse.
You can shut Him up for a fool,
you can spit at Him and kill Him as a demon;
or you can fall at his feet and call Him
Lord and God.
But let us not come with any patronizing
nonsense about his being a great human teacher.
He has not left that open to us.
He did not intend to." ♋

—C.S. Lewis from *Mere Christianity*

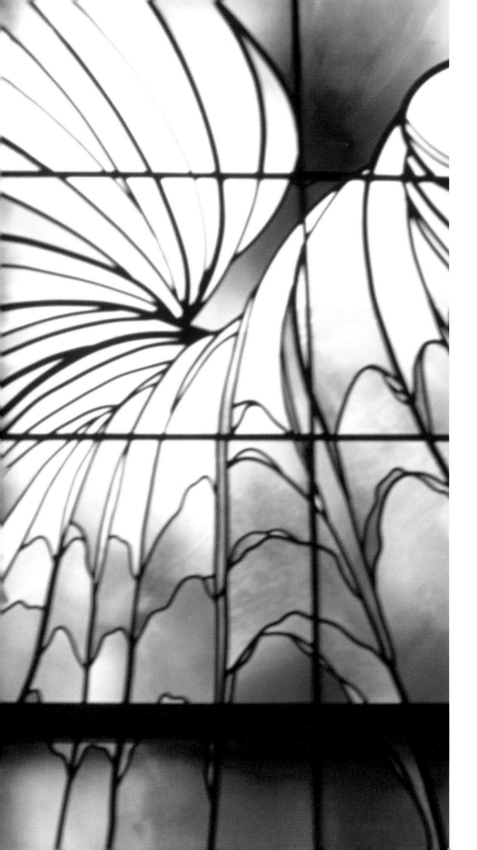

When We Meet In
Heaven

"*I*magine the meeting of the firstborn. A gathering of all God's children. No jealousy. No competition. No division. No hurry. We will be perfect . . . sinless. No more stumbles. No more tripping. Lusting will cease. Gossip will be silenced. Grudges forever removed. And imagine seeing God. Finally, to gaze in the face of your Father. To feel the Father's gaze upon you. Neither will ever cease."

—Max Lucado from *When God Whispers Your Name*

"*This is our inconsolable longing—to know and to be known.*"

—John Eldredge

"*To forgive is costly, but not to forgive is much more costly.*"

—Charles Swindoll

"He gives strength to the weary and increases the power of the weak. Even youths grow tired and weary, and young men stumble and fall; but those who hope in the LORD will renew their strength. They will soar on wings like eagles; they will run and not grow weary, they will walk and not be faint.

—Isaiah 40:29-31

"To him who is able to keep you from falling and to present you before his glorious presence without fault and with great joy — to the only God our Savior be glory, majesty, power and authority, through Jesus Christ our Lord, before all ages, now and forevermore! *Amen*."

—Jude 24, 25

What a thought: to one day enter God's presence with great joy.

"*Where is the Life we have lost in living?*"

—T.S. Eliot

"*Since an idol is not God, no matter how sincerely or passionately it is treated as God, it is bound to break the heart of its worshipper, soon or later.*"

—Peter Kreeft

"*. . . In love He [God] claims all.*"

—C.S. Lewis from *The Weight of Glory*

"*Man's answer is 'try',*
God's answer is 'trust.'"

—Peter Kreeft

"*Let us fix our eyes on Jesus, the author and perfector of our faith, who for the joy set before him, endured the cross, scorning its shame, and sat down at the right hand of the throne of God.*"

—Hebrews 12:2

Most of us can endure anything if we know there is a light at the end of the tunnel. For Jesus it was the hope and joy of Heaven.

LIVING OUT OF A
BASE OF FEAR

"... *O*ur lives are not a random series of events; they tell a Story that has meaning. We aren't in a movie we've arrived at twenty minutes late; we are in a Sacred Romance. There really is something wonderful that draws our heart; we are being wooed. But there is also something fearful. We face an enemy with vile intentions. Is anyone in charge? Someone strong and kind who notices us? At some point we have all answered that question 'no' and go on to live in a smaller story. But the answer is '*yes*'—there is someone strong and kind who notices us. Our story is written by God who is more than author, he is the romantic lead in our personal dramas. He created us for himself and now he is moving heaven and earth to restore us to his side. . . he seeks to free our heart from the attachments and addictions we've chosen . . ." ◌

—John Eldredge from *The Sacred Romance*

John Eldredge's book, "*The Sacred Romance*", is profound. Briefly stated, he tells how most of us start off with a fairy tale view of life, that life will be wonderful and that we will live happily ever after. Then, he says, the arrows of life start to come. They pierce the heart and they shatter the dreams. What then begins to happen is that we start to live out of a base of fear: "When is the next arrow coming?" However, if we believe that God is the author of our story, the *sacred romance* if you please, then we already know there will be a happy ending to the story. Rather than living from one fear to the next we can begin to live out of a base of hope because God is the divine author. ◌

Finding Peace

Scripture has much to say about finding peace. Here are some key passages:

"Let the peace of Christ rule in your hearts."
—Colossians 3:15a

"Great peace have they who love your law [Bible]."
—Psalm 119:165a [bracket, mine]

"You will keep in perfect peace him whose mind is steadfast, because he trusts in you."
—Isaiah 26:3

"Peace I leave with you; my peace I give you . . . Do not let your hearts be troubled and do not be afraid."
—John 14:27

"I have told you these things, so that in me you may have peace. In this world you will have trouble. But take heart! I have overcome the world."
—John 16:33

". . .the mind controlled by the Spirit is life and peace."
—Romans 8:6b

"May the God of hope fill you with all joy and peace as you trust in him, so that you may overflow with hope by the power of the Holy Spirit."
—Romans 15:13

"For he [Christ] himself is our peace."
—Ephesians 2:14a

"Do not be anxious about anything, but in everything, by prayer and petition, with thanksgiving, present your requests to God. And the peace of God, which transcends all understanding will guard your hearts and your minds in Christ Jesus"
—Philippians 4:6,7

"*Our lives are an extension of what we think about God.*"

—Unknown

"*Finally, brothers, whatever is true...noble...right...pure...lovely...admirable —if anything is excellent or praiseworthy —think about such things.*"

—Philippians 4:8

BAPTIST HUMOR

There were two cousins who had each gone into the ministry. One was pastor of a large metropolitan church, while the other cousin pastored a small country Baptist church. The city cousin decided to take a week's vacation and visit his country cousin. As he arrived and got out of his car, he automatically locked his car doors. The country cousin kidded him, that he was in God's country, and there was no need to lock his doors. Later that evening as they were preparing to go to bed, the city cousin, without thinking, locked the front door of the house. Again, the country cousin kidded him about how safe things were and that they weren't in the practice of locking their home. Finally, Sunday rolled around and as the two cousins arrived at the small country church the city cousin noticed that when his country cousin got out of the car he locked his car doors. He said, "Wait a minute. I thought you said this was God's country, that things are safe here. Surely, if any place should be safe it should be a church parking lot. Why did you lock your car?" The country cousin replied, "I've learned the hard way that if I don't lock the car I'll come out after church and my whole car will be filled with zucchini and squash."

There's a story told about a lone cowboy who went to an evening service at a little country Baptist church up in Montana. There was a snow storm and the only two people who showed up were the preacher and the cowboy. They waited and waited. Finally the preacher said, "Well, I guess we might as well go on home, it doesn't look like anyone else is going to show up." The cowboy responded, "Now preacher, when I go out to feed cattle, and only one cow shows up, I still feed her!" The preacher said "Okay," and proceeded to preach an hour long sermon. After it was over the cowboy said, "Preacher, that was a good sermon, but you know, when I feed cattle, and only one cow shows up, I don't give her the whole load!"

A Baptist is marooned on an island for a couple of years. When they finally find him they ask him where the other people are. He tells them he is the only one there. They ask, "But why do you have three huts?" He replies, "The first one is my house, the second one is my church, and the third one is the church I used to go to." ❧

"*You will fill me with joy in your presence, with eternal pleasures at your right hand.*"

—Psalm 16:11b

"*It is impossible to hope for that which you do not desire.*"

—John Eldredge

"Edward, it's going to be OK!"

I once had a patient whose husband's real name was "Edward." He said that only once in his entire life had his wife called him "Edward," and that was when they said their wedding vows. Otherwise, she affectionately called him "Ed," or "Eddie." However, as she was dying she looked directly at him and said, *"Edward, it's going to be OK!!"* He said she then looked up past him up toward the ceiling and her face broke into the biggest smile one can possibly imagine, and then she died. He said that he doesn't know what she saw, but that whenever he gets depressed he thinks about her face!

C.S. Lewis once wrote, "In the end that Face which is the delight or the terror of the universe must be turned upon each of us either with one expression or with the other, either conferring glory inexpressible or inflicting shame that can never be cured or disguised. I read in a periodical the other day that the fundamental thing is how we think of God. By God Himself , it is not! How God thinks of us is not only more important, but infinitely more important. Indeed how we think of Him is of no importance except insofar as it is related to how He thinks of us . . . To please God . . . to be a real ingredient in the divine happiness . . . to be loved by God, not merely pitied, but delighted in as an artist delights in his work or a father in a son—it seems impossible, a weight or burden of glory which our thoughts can hardly sustain. But so it is." [from *The Weight of Glory*]

The Apostle Paul said, "Now we see but a poor reflection as in a mirror, then we shall see face to face." What joy! What hope. Most of us can endure the hard things of life if we know there is a light at the end of the tunnel. Without that sense of hope there is only despair. When Jesus faced death the Bible says, "Who [Jesus] for the joy set before him endured the cross." (Hebrews 12:2) As long as we have the hope and joy of heaven set before us, if we know that we shall see the loving face of our Heavenly Father, it gives us the courage to keep pressing on toward our high calling in Christ. ❧

"*He who knows you the best, loves you the most.*"

—Josh McDowell

"The One I Feed The *Most*"

The story is told of a native witch doctor who had done much evil in his life, causing much needless suffering through his witchcraft. As a result of the love and work of some Christian missionaries, he yielded his heart to Christ. Later, he called a tribal meeting to share with his village the transformation that had occurred in his life. He said that before he came to know Christ, it was as though there was an evil dog in him that made him do cruel, hateful things. When he repented, and asked Christ into his life, he said it was as though a powerful dog of love and peace came to live in him.

As he spoke, a small lad sitting at his feet grew more and more absorbed with what he was saying. When the lad couldn't take the suspense any longer, he blurted out, "Did the bad dog leave?" The former witch doctor paused and said, "No, son, he still hangs around." The boy asked "How do the two dogs get along?" The old man replied, "They fight all the time." The little boy, with great concern in his voice said, "Well, which one wins?" The old man, with a smile and a twinkle in his eyes said, "The one I feed the most!" ೞ

"*He is no fool who gives what he cannot keep, to gain what he cannot lose.*"

—Jim Elliot

Jim Elliot was martyred by a tribe of head hunters in the jungles of Ecuador. His wife, Elisabeth, later went back to that same tribe and saw many of them come to faith in Christ, including the men who killed her husband. A movie has now been made of their story, entitled, "End Of The Spear."

Pray
WHEN YOU FEEL USELESS

Often, it seems, my patients feel useless. Many are bed-bound. They feel that their lives are about over, and that they are of no use to anyone. They might as well be dead. I tell them, "That's not true. You're not useless. There is one thing that you can do, and that is pray." I tell them they have time which many of us don't have; that the prayers they pray will long outlive them. If they want to invest in the future of their family, church, nation, and those they love, then pray. ❧

We Live On *Holy* Ground

My first year as a hospice chaplain was very hard emotionally. Prior to hospice I had worked in psychiatric hospitals. I was used to dealing with emotional pain, but I was not used to dealing with death. I still remember going into work one Monday morning, and our office manager very casually saying, *"Oh, by the way, Mr. Smith, Mr. Jones, and Mr. Nelson all passed away this weekend."* I felt like I had been kicked in the stomach. It almost took my breath away, for these three men were patients I had known for months. [Names changed to protect confidentiality.]

During this same time in my life I was taking a chaplaincy course at a local hospital. I shared with my chaplain supervisor how horribly I felt, losing not only these three patients, but numerous other patients, all in such a short period of time.

My supervisor reminded me of a story I'd shared with him, a story told by Zig Ziglar, about a woman who had terminal cancer. The woman's daughter said, *"Mom, if you get to Heaven, and all the stuff they say about God and Jesus is really true, would you send me a single red rose to let me know."* The mother asked, *"How am I to do that?"* The daughter responded, *"God can do anything."*

They agreed that it would be a secret between the two of them, and they would not share it with a soul.—A few weeks later at the funeral the daughter had forgotten about the rose, when a stranger walked into sanctuary, walked down the aisle, and placed a single red rose on top of the casket. Following the ceremony, the daughter went up to him and asked why he had done that. He said, *"Honey, it was the strangest thing, but all day long I couldn't get it out of my mind, I had to bring a single red rose!"*

My supervisor, knowing this story, said, *"Close your eyes. Now visualize taking single red roses and place one on each of the ten caskets of the ten patients you knew who died."*—When I went through that little exercise I was expecting to feel a lot of loss and sadness. To my surprise, the overwhelming feeling that hit me was that I had been walking on *holy ground.*—And it is true. It doesn't get a whole lot closer between Heaven and earth than at a dying person's bedside.

Once I received a call from the family of a very close friend of mine, a woman whose husband had been a patient of mine. I had even preached her husband's funeral. His wife had gone in for a routine surgery when tragedy hit. She had internal bleeding and they had to do a second surgery to stop the bleeding. Her body wasn't strong enough and she went into a coma and was actively dying when I arrived at the Intensive Care Unit. The family made the hard decision to take her off life support.

I had everyone in the room share any last words of love with her, as though she could hear. [Hearing is the last thing to go when a patient is dying.] Following the goodbyes, everyone left the room except the doctor, two nurses, and myself. They took her off life-support and then they left me alone with her. For the last 10-15 minutes of her life I held her hand and prayed for her as she went to be with the Lord. It was one of the most sacred moments of my entire life. I truly believe I had been on *holy ground.* ❧

Holy Ground

"*Marriage heals this. Jointly the two become fully human…And then one or other dies. And we think of this as love cut short; like a dance stopped in mid-career…I can't help suspecting, the dead also feel the pains of separation…bereavement is a universal and integral part of our experience of love. It follows marriage as normally as marriage follows courtship.*"

—C.S. Lewis from *A Grief Observed*, writing about his wife's death.

"'For I know the plans I have for you,'
declares the LORD, 'plans to prosper you
and not to harm you, plans to
give you hope and a future.
Then you will call upon me and
come and pray to me, and I will listen to
you. You will seek me and find me
when you seek me with all your heart.'"

—Jeremiah 29:11-13

"The LORD is righteous in all his
ways and loving toward all he has made.
The LORD is near to all who call on him,
to all who call on him in truth. He fulfills
the desires of those who fear him..."

—Psalm 145:17-19

"My grace is sufficient for you, for my power is made perfect in weakness."

—II Corinthians 12:9

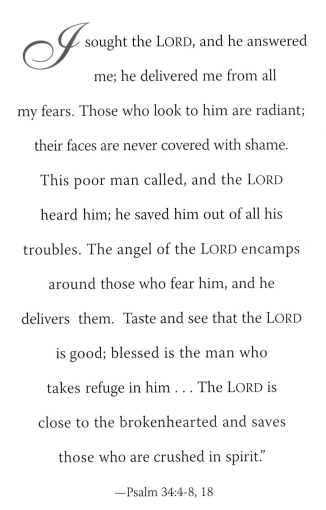

I sought the LORD, and he answered me; he delivered me from all my fears. Those who look to him are radiant; their faces are never covered with shame. This poor man called, and the LORD heard him; he saved him out of all his troubles. The angel of the LORD encamps around those who fear him, and he delivers them. Taste and see that the LORD is good; blessed is the man who takes refuge in him . . . The LORD is close to the brokenhearted and saves those who are crushed in spirit."

—Psalm 34:4-8, 18

"*Y*ou cannot outdream God."

—John Eldredge

"*Seek* the LORD while he may be found; call upon him while he is near."

—Isaiah 55:6

"*We shall never exhaust the wonder, the dazzlingly enthralling drinking of limitless Beauty. Indeed, 'eye has not seen, nor ear heard, nor can we even imagine what God has prepared for those who love him.' (I Corinthians 2:9) ... Heaven is eternal ecstasy.*"

—Thomas Dubay from
The Evidential Power of Beauty

" *We* are like an ant at the base of Mt. Everest, so focused on our little anthill that we miss the bigger picture, namely God and eternity."

—Bart Larson

"*Now to him who is able to do immeasurably more than all we ask or imagine, according to his power that is at work within us...*"

—Ephesians 3:20

" *If you think of this world as a place intended simply for our happiness, you find it quite intolerable: think of it as a place of training and correction and it's not so bad.*"

—C.S. Lewis from *God In The Dock*

154

"So, why are we bored? Why this distinctively modern phenomenon? The very word for it did not exist in premodern languages!... how do we explain the irony that the very society which for the first time in history has conquered by technology and turned the world into a giant fun-and-game factory, a rich kid's playroom, the very society which has the least reason to be bored, is the most bored?

There is only one thing which never gets boring: God."

—Peter Kreeft

"*God*...is the source from which all your reasoning power comes: you could not be right and He wrong any more than a stream can rise higher than its own source."

—C.S. Lewis from *Mere Christianity*

"*R*ather than question the severity of God in allowing suffering, maybe we should instead question the severity of sin that would cause a loving God to go to such extremes to get our attention and show us the serious consequence of our choices. Sin, unchecked, would reap compound dividends for all eternity. It is His severe mercy that He sometimes intervenes and stops us in our tracks by means of suffering. Love and justice demand no less." ❧

Thoughts from the book
"The Goodness Of God"

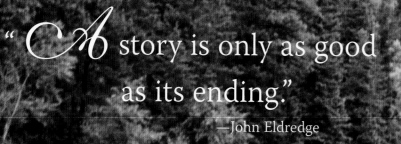

"$\mathcal{A}$ story is only as good as its ending."

—John Eldredge

"*Jesus said to her, 'I am the resurrection and the life. He who believes in me will live, even though he dies; and whoever lives and believes in me will never die.'*"

—John 11:25-26

CHAPLAIN'S PRAYER

Gracious Lord,

As I begin this day of ministering to the needs of others, may I see with your eyes, and love with your compassion. I humbly acknowledge that I am not up to the task before me. I need the filling and empowering of your Spirit if I am to genuinely love and care for those I meet. Teach me to quiet my heart, to spend quality time with you before I rush into this day; that I may minister to others out of a cup that *runneth over,* not from an empty well.

Grant that I may listen and hear the true heart-felt needs of my patients and their families. May I not be so wrapped up in myself, and my own issues, that I fail to meet people where they are emotionally and spiritually. Give me the courage to come from my heart and not just my head. May my words be few, and may they be words of truth, empathy, and hope spoken in love. I pray that each person to whom I minister will be brought at least one step closer to you because of my being with them.

I believe you are the Great Shepherd. As I point others to you, I thank you that you long to lead and shepherd them; whether beside the still waters, or through the valley of the shadow of death. Draw to the fold those who do not know you. Teach them to hear your gentle voice. I pray that I, along with them, may come to know your unfailing love, faithfulness, and presence.

I pray that you will sovereignly lead me to the patients, family and staff you want me to visit today. May I do no more, nor no less, than you ask of me, and may my attitude reflect yours.

I thank you for the gift of life. May I never take it for granted. Where I fail you, forgive me; for I too stand in need of your mercy and grace. Make me an instrument of your grace, and when others see me, may the light of your countenance be upon my face.

I pray these things in the name of our blessed Lord and Savior,

—Amen.